STUDY GUIDE

Volume I: To 1550

THE EARTH AND ITS PEOPLES
A GLOBAL HISTORY
SECOND EDITION

STUDY GUIDE

Volume I: To 1550

Michele G. Scott James
MiraCosta College

THE EARTH AND ITS PEOPLES
A GLOBAL HISTORY
SECOND EDITION

Richard W. Bulliet
Columbia University

Pamela Kyle Crossley
Dartmouth College

Daniel R. Headrick
Roosevelt University

Steven W. Hirsch
Tufts University

Lyman L. Johnson
University of North Carolina – Charlotte

David Northrup
Boston College

HOUGHTON MIFFLIN COMPANY   BOSTON   NEW YORK

Sponsoring Editor: Nancy Blaine
Editorial Associate: Gillie Jones
Manufacturing Coordinator: Marie Barnes
Marketing Manager: Sandra McGuire

Thanks again, Del, Jacob, Gina, and Kelsey.

Printed in the U.S.A.

ISBN: 0-618-00081-X

23456789-VG-04 03 02 01 00

Contents

To the Student

Welcome to world history. Whether this is your first history course or you are a history major, you will enjoy the vast scope and quick pace of world history. You will be learning a great deal about the earth and its peoples in one class. Because there is a large amount of information, it helps to be organized right from the beginning. Part of your study system should be the completion of this *Study Guide*.

How to Use This Study Guide

Read the chapter objectives in *The Earth and Its Peoples: A Global History*; then read the entire chapter.

Highlight or underline important facts or words. Do *not* underline too much of the text; underline only key words and phrases so that you can find them when you review.

Fill in the blank *outline* provided for you in the *Study Guide*. Included are the large subject headings to keep you on track. You may not need to fill in all the lines, or you may find yourself adding lines. That's okay. The outline is designed to help you learn the structure and important themes of the chapter.

Then fill in the *identifications* section. It contains the key terms listed at the end of each chapter, plus a few additional terms, names, and concepts that you need to learn in order to master the material. To answer an identification question, define the term; provide relevant date or dates; and tell why the term is significant. If you leave out any of this information on a test, you will probably not receive full credit, even if what you have written is correct.

Next, test yourself on the *multiple-choice questions*. Many professors like to test a student's recall of facts and so will use multiple-choice questions. However, even if your professor does not give multiple-choice tests, you will find that if you do well on this section, it will improve your overall performance.

The *short-answer questions* resemble the identifications in that you should define the term, event, or concept, then give a date, and explain the significance. Three to five sentences is usually sufficient to answer such a question.

Essay questions are probably the most difficult type of question that students must deal with. The key to answering them successfully is to be organized. First outline the major themes that you will use to answer the question. Then assemble the details, including dates, that you will need to support your themes. When you have them all together, you can begin to write your essay. Write formally, using complete sentences, good grammar and style, and correct spelling. Always reread your essays, both to make any needed corrections and to ensure that you have answered the question completely.

Comparison charts allow you to make comparisons between societies, time periods, peoples, and philosophies. Be guided by the chart title and chapter content for hints on how to complete each chart. Fill in all the blank areas that you can. These charts will aid you in class discussions, essays, and perhaps even term papers.

The *Society and Culture* sections allow you to critically examine a primary document created by people who lived in the past. The Study Guide contains some questions that supplement those in the text. By reading the primary documents, and answering the questions, you will have a unique ability to see the past through the eyes of individuals who lived long ago.

The *Internet Assignment* section will allow you to view at least two relevant images from each chapter. Use your favorite browser to look up the keywords listed and then analyze each image. Questions are provided to help you interpret what you are viewing. Your instructor has a list of the images, and may use them in class discussion or in assignments or tests. Here, as well as in your research assignments, you may want to rely on college or university sites (these often contain "edu" in the address) and well-established sites such as PBS.org or Discovery.com. Some of the images may be found in the *History WIRED* image library on the Bulliet, *The Earth and Its Peoples* website. To locate the Bulliet home page, begin at the Houghton Mifflin college site (http://college.hmco.com) and select "history" from the available disciplines. Once you have located the history homepage, select *The Earth and Its Peoples* from the books listed to visit *History WIRED*, as well as a wealth of other resources.

Internet Exploration offers some less conventional websites and keywords designed to stretch and challenge the boundaries of history and the teaching of history. Many keywords and sites will lead you to virtual tours, games, and sites containing controversial theories. History is constantly changing, and new theories rise all of the time. Using the keywords and websites listed in each chapter will expose you to new ideas, and things you may never have thought of as history.

Maps help you visualize the geographic region in which the historical events you are studying took place, thus increasing your understanding of these events. Because many professors give map quizzes or include geography questions on tests, the *map exercises* at the end of each chapter will help you prepare to answer such questions. Feel free to use different colors and patterns to shade in regions and plot map points on the blank maps provided with the exercises.

Ten Quick Tips for Doing Well in Your World History Class

1. Attend all the classes and take careful notes.

2. Read your textbook chapter attentively. Remember that many professors require students to read the text before class. Don't get behind on the reading and don't put off catching up until late in the term.

3. Complete your *Study Guide.*

4. Spend some quiet, uninterrupted time each week really learning the material, not just reading over the text.

5. After you finish each chapter, read over your lecture notes and *Study Guide* outline.

6. Get together with your classmates and form study groups.

7. Get enough sleep and eat a good meal before your test.

8. Don't cram before an examination. If you like, you can read over your notes just before a test, but don't try to learn new material. Instead, concentrate on the material you already know.

9. Relax, word hard, and do your best.

10. History is fun—so enjoy yourself!

Why Study History?

Each of us walked with Lucy at Hadar. Each of us was a soldier in Napoleon's army, a Chinese princess, an artist painting the walls of the cave at Lascaux, an Olmec astronomer, a follower of the Buddha, a pilgrim traveling with Mansa Kankan Musa, a suffragist marching for the vote of women, and a Polynesian navigator. Since we are all each of these people, history belongs to us; it is our participation in the human experience.

We study history because it teaches us about the nature of humanity. Studying history is not merely learning what we have done in the past; it is studying who we are. It leads us to understand and cherish the vast range of human experience and so helps us recognize the value of diversity. It encourages us to look up from our daily lives toward a larger world and to appreciate the role we play in that world—the role we play in history.

STUDY GUIDE

Volume I: To 1500

THE EARTH AND ITS PEOPLES
A GLOBAL HISTORY
SECOND EDITION

CHAPTER 1

Nature, Humanity, and History: The First Four Million Years

Learning Objectives

After reading Chapter 1 and completing this study chapter, you should be able to explain:

- How early human development may have taken place, and what physical and technological advances human beings made along the way.

- How human beings began to depend on lifestyle changes rather than on biological evolution to adapt to new environments.

- How Homo erectus and Homo sapiens began to migrate over the face of the earth, and how certain technologies, such as fire, facilitated those moves.

- Why the evolution from hunting and gathering marks one of the most momentous changes in all of human history, and what was involved in this complex process.

- What life was like in Neolithic communities as people began to settle down, build large cities, specialize in professions, and develop new outlooks on society and religion.

Chapter Outline

In the outline below, include important themes, concepts, and details in the blank spaces provided. If you find fewer points than you have space for, leave lines blank. If you find more points, add as many lines as necessary.

   I. Introduction

       A. *Creation Myths—Various Themes*

          1. *From the sky—Yoruba (Africa)*

          2. *Hole in the ground*

   3.   *Adam and Eve—Hebrew Bible*

B.   *Purpose of Creation Myths*

   1.   *Define moral principles of a society*

   2.   *Guide dealings with nature and supernatural*

   3.   *Explain human social systems and daily life*

C.   *Nineteenth Century—Impact of Science on Creation Myths*

   1.   *Physical evidence to support evolution of plants and animals*

   2.   *Human beings here much longer than we used to think*

   3.   *People have developed gradually for many hundreds of thousands of years in response to their environment*

II.   African Genesis

A.   *Interpreting the Evidence*

   1.   *Neanderthal—40,000 yrs. ago—Europe*

      a.   *discovered in 1856 by German workers*

      b.   *Scholars at first thought they were deformed modern people—not ancient beings*

      c.   _____

   2.   *Charles Darwin*

      a.   *On the Origin of Species (1859) and The Descent of Man (1871)*

      b.   *Biological life around a lot longer than we thought—biological variation*

      c.   *Natural selection—biological variations enhance species' survival—sometimes new species*

      d.   *African origin of human beings—"descended from a hairy, tailed quadruped"*

   3.   *Australopithecus africanus (African southern ape)*

      a.   *Raymond Dart argued transitional between apes and humans*

      b.   *Leakeys—excavated Great Rift Valley of E. Africa*

      c.   *Archaeologists sift through material—dating methods*

B. *Human Evolution*

    1.   *How should humans be defined? Hominids in the primate family*

        a.   *Warm-blooded, furry, four limbs, mammals—social—65 million yrs. ago*

        b.   *Humans most closely related to chimps and gorillas*

        c.   *98% of DNA shared with apes*

    2.   *Three major traits distinguish humans from other primates*

        a.   *First to appear—bipedalism, which freed forelimbs—thumb can work with fingers for manipulation*

        b.   *Large brain—abstract thinking, profound emotions, complex social relations, fine motor movements*

        c.   *Physical possibility for speech—larynx (voice box)*

    3.   *Why did biological changes take place?*

        a.   *Certain genetic changes enhanced survival*

        b.   *Evolution caused by shifts in world climate—Ice Age (Pleistocene epoch) 2 million to 11,000 yrs. ago*

        c.   *Donald Johanson (1974)—Lucy—northern Ethiopia (?human)*

        d.   *Olduvai Gorge—Homo habilis (handy human)—2 to 3 million yrs. ago, brain 50% larger than australopithecine*

        e.   *1.8 million yrs. ago—Homo erectus (upright human)—brain a third larger than brain of Homo habilis*

        f.   *400,000 to 100,000 yrs. ago—Homo sapiens (wise human)—brain a third larger than brain of Homo erectus*

C. *Migrations from Africa*

    1.   *Homo erectus*

        a.   *First humans to live all over Africa*

b.   *Went to southern Asia—land bridge to Java 1.8 million yrs. ago*

c.   *Went to northern Europe and northern China 700,000 to 300,000 yrs. ago*

2.   *Homo sapiens—spread out from Africa*

a.   *Wet weather in Sahara helped migrations until 40,000 yrs. ago—population increase*

b.   *Abundance of food, population increase—Homo sapiens sapiens (modern human)*

c.   *Displaced older populations—crossed land bridge to Americas 32,000 to 13,000 yrs. ago*

3.   *Minor evolutionary changes*

a.   *Skin color—dark skin reduces sun damage, pale skin allows more vitamin D absorption*

b.   *Didn't make major physical adaptations—dispersed populations of humans vary little*

c.   *Instead they changed their habits*

III.   History and Culture in the Ice Age

A.   *Food Gathering and Stone Technology*

1.   *Food gathering*

a.   *Vegetable foods made up bulk of diet*

b.   *Ice Age hunting became more common—meat for feasts*

c.   *Hunting connected to toolmaking*

2.   *Toolmaking—stone—2 million to 4,000 yrs. ago*

a.   *First recognizable cultural activity*

b.   *Tools made from stone, bones, skins, and wood*

c.   *Effective for hunting and butchering*

3.   *The hunters*

    c. *Middle East, 8000 B.C.E.; North Africa, 8000 B.C.E.; Nile, 5000 B.C.E.; Greece, 6000 B.C.E.; Europe, 4000 B.C.E.; Asia 10,000 (?)—5000 B.C.E.; Mexico 3500 B.C.E.*

B. *Animal Domestication and Pastoralism*

    1. *Domesticated animals provided meat, milk, & energy—Middle East*

        a. *After 7000 B.C.E. gradual decline of wild gazelle bones in refuse piles—overhunting*

        b. *Same refuse piles had sheep and goat bones replacing gazelle bones*

        c. *People probably fed tamer animals foraging for food in trash heaps—domestication*

    2. *Selective breeding final step of domestication*

        a. *Desirable characteristics—high milk yield, long wool*

        b. *China—pigs and water buffalo; India—pigs, cattle, buffalo; Americas—llamas*

        c. *Used for food, fertilizer, and clothes*

    3. *Mixed farming and herding*

        a. *Americas—llamas, guinea pigs, fowls, maize, squash*

        b. *Africa and Central Asia—milk, not meat—bartered for vegetables*

        c.

C. *Agriculture and Ecological Crisis*

    1. *Why turn to agriculture?*

        a. *Enough grain to brew beer*

        b. *Ecological crisis—global warming—why so many people adopted agriculture at once*

        c. *Crisis may have been a shortage of wild food—warmer and wetter climate, or population increase*

    2. *In many areas of the world people continued to hunt and gather—no agriculture*

       a.   *Australia—hunting and gathering until recently*

       b.   *Amerindians—hunting bison, salmon fishing, catching shellfish—settled down*

       c.   *Southern Africa—retained old ways, Eurasia—reindeer-based*

    3.   *Agriculture adopted 10,000 to 2,000 yrs. ago—momentous impact*

       a.   *100,000 yrs. ago, 2 million people—temperate and tropical regions*

       b.   *5000 B.C.E., 10 million people*

       c.   *1000 B.C.E., 50 million to 100 million people*

V. Life in Neolithic Communities

    A.   *Rural Population and Settlement*

       1.   *Violent or peaceful transition?*

          a.   *Violence as farmers cleared land—took away hunting ground?*

          b.   *Process was probably gradual displacement*

          c.

       2.   *Why could they expand?*

          a.   *Small surpluses gave long-term advantage in population growth and survival*

          b.   *Farming areas spread as population grew—wild areas shrank gradually*

          c.   *Evidence supporting spread: gene mapping in Europe*

       3.   *Communities organized around kinship and marriage*

          a.   *Clans and lineages the basis of land ownership*

          b.   *Matriarchal—tracing descent through female line—sometimes—no evidence for matriarchy*

          c.   *Patriarchal society—tracing descent through male line common*

    B.   *Cultural Expressions*

       1.   *Religion—ancestors—earth—sky—used all*

    a.   *Burials and ancestor cults (megaliths and ziggurats)*

    b.   *Agriculture—Earth Mother—source of all new life*

    c.   *Male Sky God—all powerful*

  2.   *Language diffusion—supposition—we don't know what people spoke in Neolithic*

    a.   *Indo-European languages and migrations*

    b.   *Afro-Asiatic languages and migrations*

    c.   *Sino-Tibetan spread*

  3.   _____

    a.   _____

    b.   _____

    c.   _____

C.   *Early Towns and Specialists*

  1.   *Villages grew into towns—farmers*

    a.   *Centers of trade & craft specialization*

    b.   *Elaborate houses and temples, food surpluses*

    c.   *Craft specialists—spent time making things—not needed to grow food*

  2.   *8000 B.C.E.—Jericho*

    a.   *10-acre settlement—mud houses*

    b.   *Massive stone wall—defense against invasion*

    c.   _____

  3.   *7000–5000 B.C.E.—Çatal Hüyük*

    a.   *32 acres—mud houses—elaborately decorated*

    b.   *No defensive wall—but outer houses had no windows facing outside—effective barrier*

c.   *Long-distance trade and fine arts and crafts—religious artifacts*

VI. **Conclusion**

A. *Human Interaction with the Environment*

1.   *At first survival and physical adaptation*

2.   *Neolithic peoples adapted to their environments and shaped them*

3.   *Agriculture one of the most momentous changes in human history*

B. _____

1.   _____

2.   _____

3.   _____

C. _____

1.   _____

2.   _____

3.   _____

Identifications

Define each term and explain why it is significant, including any important dates.

	Identification	*Significance*
Charles Darwin		
natural selection		
evolution		
australopithecines		
hominid		

	Identification	*Significance*
bipedalism		
Great Ice Age		
Homo habilis		
Homo erectus		
Homo sapiens		
culture		
history		
tools		
Stone Age		
Paleolithic		
Neolithic		
forager		
agricultural revolutions		
lineages and clans		
Holocene		
megalith		
Çatal Hüyük		

Multiple-Choice Questions

Read the entire question, including *all* the possible answers. Then choose the *one* answer that best fits the question.

1. Creation myths generally do *not*
   a. define the moral principles of society.
   b. record actual historical events for posterity.
   c. set up the guidelines for human dealings with the supernatural world.
   d. explain how a people's way of life and cultural system arose.

2. The physical and mental abilities that Homo sapiens sapiens gradually acquired gave these human beings the capacity to adapt to new environments by
   a. evolving new physical attributes to keep from becoming extinct.
   b. altering their way of life rather than by evolving physically as do other species.
   c. both by major physical evolution and change of lifestyle.
   d. not changing at all.

3. Evolutionists believe that
   a. humans are descended from apes.
   b. humans and apes are not closely related.
   c. humans and apes are both descended from a hairy, tailed quadruped.
   d. apes only are descended from a hairy, tailed quadruped.

4. Naturalists first surmised that humans originated in
   a. Africa.
   b. Asia.
   c. America.
   d. Australia.

5. Within the primate kingdom, humans are most closely related to
   a. lemurs.
   b. the small hairy, tailed creatures from which they are descended.
   c. chimpanzees.
   d. baboons.

6. Homo sapiens means
   a. handy human.
   b. upright human.
   c. wise human.
   d. nearly human.

7. Why is the name "Stone Age" misleading?
   a. It implies that people lived in stone dwellings.
   b. People used tools made out of many things, not just stone.
   c. Stone tools have been used throughout all of human history.
   d. People did not use stone tools during this time.

8. Which of the following traits does *not* describe hunting and gathering bands?
    a. They must have at least fifty people in them to adequately provide for themselves.
    b. They must remain highly mobile to follow herds.
    c. Men usually hunt and women usually gather.
    d. Some scholars think that early human bands may have resembled bands of chimpanzees or gorillas.

9. Which of the following did *not* encourage the shift away from the mother-centered family to the development of the two-parent family?
    a. Human offspring take up to fifteen years to mature and so need a great deal of supervision.
    b. Human females are physically able to mate at any time, not just during estrus, thereby encouraging the development of monogamy and emotional attachment.
    c. Labor came to be divided so that men hunted and women gathered.
    d. Because of the lack of a mating season, humans could produce more children, necessitating more caregiving.

10. About how many hours do scholars estimate it took a member of a hunting and gathering band to secure food, clothing, and shelter for that day?
    a. One to two
    b. Three to five
    c. Seven to nine
    d. Eleven to fifteen

11. Which of the following is *not* one of the theories that scholars have about why people made cave paintings?
    a. To tell time
    b. To educate their young people
    c. To predict the future (fortunetelling)
    d. To express concerns with fertility

12. Which of the following was *not* fundamental to the success of agriculture?
    a. Good tools
    b. Long-distance trade
    c. Slash-and-burn techniques
    d. High-yield strains of plants

13. The first animal to be domesticated was the
    a. dog.
    b. horse.
    c. cow.
    d. chicken.

14. Which of the following is *not* one of the reasons that people may have been drawn to agriculture?
    a. Colder weather, which meant fewer animals
    b. Ensuring themselves a ready supply of beer
    c. Shortages of wild food
    d. A rising population

15. Agriculturalists produced more specialized material goods and art because
    a. farmers had more free time than hunters and gatherers.
    b. agricultural societies had more sophisticated tastes.
    c. they were able to record how to make such things as pottery, jewelry, and metal goods using newly invented writing systems.
    d. larger communities of people could spare some members from food production for more specialized activities.

Short-Answer Questions

Answer each question in one short paragraph, giving the definition, dates, and significance.

1. Why did bipedalism evolve in humans? What advantages did it provide? Did it cause any problems?

2. Why did Europeans evolve lighter skin colors? What disadvantage did this adaptation have?

3. How old are the cave paintings at Lascaux and Vallon-Pont d'Arc and what purpose might they have had?

4. Why did peoples south of the Sahara base their farming and diet on a variety of locally domesticated grains rather than use wheat and barley?

5. Discuss the process by which animals were domesticated. How did the domestication of animals affect the lives of those who kept them?

Essay Questions

Make an outline for each question, listing the major points you want to discuss. Then write your practice essay, following your outline carefully and making sure that you do not skip any of your major points. At this time you will want to add the relevant dates and details that will make your essay persuasive and accurate.

1. What distinguishes human beings from their closest relatives, the apes? What are some similarities between them? How and why did humans evolve biologically?

2. Trace the migrations of Homo erectus and Homo sapiens. Why did they migrate? What facilitated their migrations?

3. Discuss the role of anthropology in the study of prehistoric human societies. Why is it necessary? What can we learn from it? What can't we learn from it?

4. Trace the development of agriculture. How was it invented? By whom? How did it change the lifestyles of the people who practiced it? Did it spread, or was it reinvented in different regions of the world? How did it help farming to become the dominant lifestyle of people in the world?

5. Describe Neolithic religion. What were its characteristics? What practices did it have? How were the concerns of Neolithic peoples manifested in their religion?

Comparison Charts

Using information gathered from the text, fill in the blank areas of each chart with the relevant data pertaining to the regions and categories listed. (Not all blank areas will necessarily be used.)

Chart 1.1
THE DEVELOPMENT OF MODERN HUMANS

	Dates	Physical Attributes	Brain Size	Diet	Gathering Techniques	Hunting Skills	Tools	Geographic Regions
Homo erectus								
Homo habilis								
Homo sapiens								

Chart 1.2
EVOLUTION OF HUMAN LIFESTYLES

	Approximate Dates	Population	Regions of the World	Foods	Wealth	Technology	Metals	Migrations	Social Structure/ Hierarchy	Hours Worked per Day	Religion
Hunters and Gatherers											
Pastoralists											
Agriculturalists											

Society and Culture

After reading "Society and Culture: Interpreting Rock Art" in your text, answer the following additional questions.

If you had only the drawing to go by, how would you interpret it? Why is it important to understand the cultural context in which a work of art is made? What do you know about the San that helps explain why they attached such importance to animals? Why might the San prize personal mystical experiences?

Can this picture be used to explain the curing of sickness, the control of herds, or the making of rain? There are several other figures in the picture, other than those numbered and discussed in the text; what might they be doing?

Internet Assignment

Keywords: "Lascaux"

                "Venus of Willendorf" or "Neolithic Venuses"

When studying peoples who lived before the development of writing, scholars have to depend on other types of evidence. Archaeological data makes up much of this evidence. Two famous sources on which scholars depend are the cave paintings of Lascaux and the Venus of Willendorf. Use the above keywords to find web sites about the cave paintings at Lascaux, France and the Venus of Willendorf. You might want to consult the *History WIRED* image library on the Bulliet, *The Earth and Its Peoples* web site (refer to the preface of this study guide for information on how to locate the Bulliet home page).

What can an examination of these two images tell us about the societies that created them? What things may have been important to them? How might they have made their livings? What purposes might these images have served?

Internet Exploration

Ever wondered what happens on an archaeological dig? How do archaeologists find artifacts? What can those artifacts tell us? Look up the keywords "archaeological pieces of the past" to look at some sites and get some "virtual" experience digging in the field, and finding ancient artifacts. A specific site that you may like is www.pbs.org/wgbh/nova/laventa/archaeologist.html.

Map Exercises

On Outline Map 1.1, trace the migrations of Homo erectus and Homo sapiens. Then mark the areas covered by ice sheets twenty thousand years ago.

Outline Map 1.1

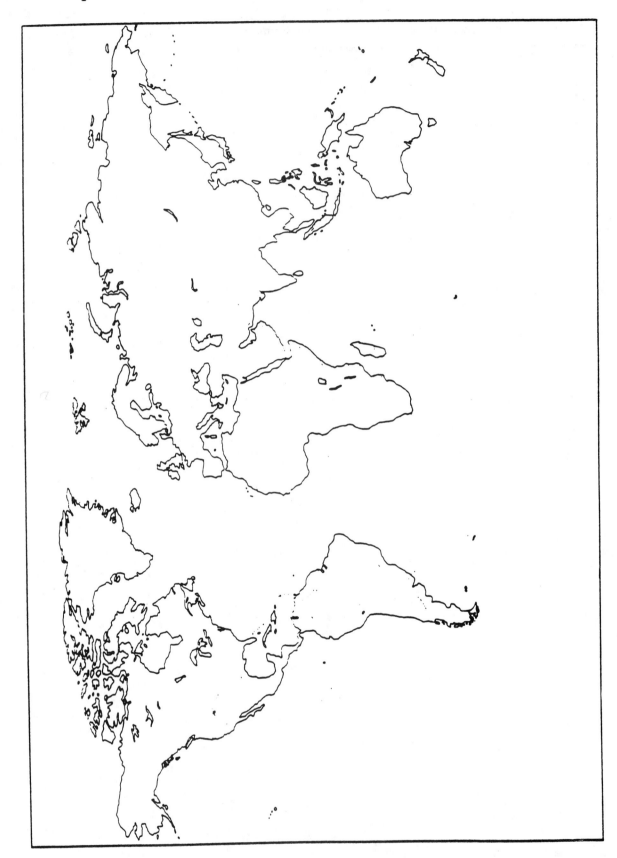

CHAPTER 2

The First River-Valley Civilizations, 3500 – 1500 B.C.E.

Learning Objectives

After reading Chapter 2 and completing this study chapter, you should be able to explain:

- Why the first civilizations tended to develop on floodplains near large rivers, and how other features of the environment influenced the political, religious, and technical development of those civilizations.

- How large-scale public works projects, such as irrigation systems and pyramids, were built with simple technology and human power.

- How the trade networks of western Eurasia and northern Africa became increasingly intertwined, and what resulted from this condition.

- What factors contribute to the downfall of civilizations, particularly those elements affecting the Indus River civilization.

Chapter Outline

In the outline below, include important themes, concepts, and details in the blank spaces provided. If you find fewer points than you have space for, leave lines blank. If you find more points, add as many lines as necessary.

I. Introduction

    A. *Mesopotamian definition of "civilization"* _____

        1. _____

        2. _____

        3. _____

B. Modern scholars' definition of civilization _____

    1. _____

    2. _____

    3. _____

C. Early civilizations in floodplains _____

    1. _____

    2. _____

    3. _____

II. Mesopotamia

A. Settled Agriculture in an Unstable Landscape _____

    1. The land lies between two rivers on an alluvial plain _____

        a. _____

        b. _____

        c. _____

    2. First domestication of plants and animals in Mesopotamia—5000 B.C.E. (8000 B.C.E. in fertile crescent) _____

        a. _____

        b. _____

        c. _____

    3. Sumerians earliest known people in Mesopotamia _____

        a. _____

        b. _____

        c. _____

B. Cities, Kings, and Trade _____

1. *Cities: purpose, evolution, and the city state* _____

    a. _____

    b. _____

    c. _____

2. *Authority: religious and secular* _____

    a. _____

    b. _____

    c. _____

3. *Trade and conquest: alternative ways to get resources* _____

    a. _____

    b. _____

    c. _____

C. *Mesopotamian Society* _____

1. *Social divisions part of civilization* _____

    a. _____

    b. _____

    c. _____

2. *Daily life hard to discover* _____

    a. _____

    b. _____

    c. _____

3. *Women in Mesopotamia* _____

    a. _____

    b. _____

c. _____

D. *Gods, Priests, and Temples* _____

    1.   *Many anthropomorphic (humanlike) gods* _____

         a. _____

         b. _____

         c. _____

    2.   *Public religion and temples* _____

         a. _____

         b. _____

         c. _____

    3.   *Priests* _____

         a. _____

         b. _____

         c. _____

    4.   *Religion of the common people* _____

         a. _____

         b. _____

         c. _____

E. *Technology and Science* _____

    1.   *Technology: any specialized knowledge that is used to transform the national environment and human society* _____

         a. _____

         b. _____

c. _____

2. *Writing* _____

   a. _____

   b. _____

   c. _____

3. *Other important technologies* _____

   a. _____

   b. _____

   c. _____

   d. _____

   e. _____

III. Egypt

A. *The Land of Egypt: "Gift of the Nile"* _____

1. *The Nile is the fundamental geographic feature of Egypt* _____

   a. _____

   b. _____

   c. _____

2. *Use of the Nile and development of agriculture* _____

   a. _____

   b. _____

   c. _____

3. *Egypt was well endowed with natural resources* _____

   a. _____

b. _____

c. _____

4. *Climatic changes led to large-scale growth* _____

a. _____

b. _____

c. _____

B. *Divine Kingship* _____

1. *Unification of all of Egypt by Menes 3100 B.C.E.* _____

a. _____

b. _____

c. _____

2. *The Pharaoh was a god come to earth* _____

a. _____

b. _____

c. _____

3. *The death of the Pharaoh and his tomb* _____

a. _____

b. _____

c. _____

C. *Administration and Communication* _____

1. *The need for good records led to a complex administrative bureaucracy and the development of writing* _____

a. _____

b. _____

c. _____

2. *Tension between capital and home districts paralleled in tension between monarchy and bureaucrats*

   a. _____

   b. _____

   c. _____

3. *Foreign policy and trade*

   a. _____

   b. _____

   c. _____

D. *The People of Egypt*

   1. *Social stratification clearly existed*

      a. _____

      b. _____

      c. _____

   2. *Lives of ordinary Egyptians and slavery*

      a. _____

      b. _____

      c. _____

   3. *Women in ancient Egypt*

      a. _____

      b. _____

      c. _____

E. *Belief and Knowledge*

1. *Religion rooted in the landscape of the Nile and the vision of cosmic order that it evoked*

   a. _____

   b. _____

   c. _____

2. *Gods were diverse in origin and nature*

   a. _____

   b. _____

   c. _____

3. *Afterlife—real and much prepared for—an obsession really*

   a. _____

   b. _____

   c. _____

IV. **The Indus Valley Civilization**

   A. *Natural Environment*

   1. *The Indus River*

      a. _____

      b. _____

      c. _____

   2. *Cultivation*

      a. _____

      b. _____

      c. _____

   3. *Several adjacent regions shared cultural attributes with the core area*

      a. _____

     b. _____

     c. _____

B. *Material Culture* _____

   1. *Identity, origin, and fate of the people of Indus society are in dispute*

     a. _____

     b. _____

     c. _____

   2. *Indus was a very urban society*

     a. _____

     b. _____

     c. _____

   3. *Technology and trade*

     a. _____

     b. _____

     c. _____

   4. *We know little about the political, social, economic, and religious structures*

     a. _____

     b. _____

     c. _____

C. *Transformation of the Indus Valley Civilization* _____

   1. *Indus Valley cities abandoned 1900 B.C.E.*

     a. _____

     b. _____

c. _____

2. *"Systems failure"* _____

    a. _____

    b. _____

    c. _____

3. *Gradual ecological changes* _____

    a. _____

    b. _____

    c. _____

V. Conclusion

A. *No accident that these civilizations were in river valleys* _____

    1. _____

    2. _____

    3. _____

B. *Mesopotamian environment affected attitude and religion* _____

    1. _____

    2. _____

    3. _____

C. *The predictability of the Egyptian environment encouraged trust in gods* _____

    1. _____

    2. _____

    3. _____

Identifications

Define each term and explain why it is significant, including any important dates.

	Identification	*Significance*
civilization		
floodplains		
Babylon		
Sumerians		
Semitic		
city-state		
Hammurabi		
scribe		
ziggurat		
writing		
technology		
irrigation		
Nubia		
amulet		
cuneiform		
pharaoh		

	Identification	*Significance*
ma'at		
pyramid		
Memphis		
Thebes		
hieroglyphics		
papyrus		
mummy		
mathematics		
Harappa		
Mohenjo-Daro		
systems failure		

Multiple-Choice Questions

Read the entire question, including *all* the possible answers. Then choose the *one* answer that best fits the question.

1. Which of the following attributes is *not* essential to the definition of civilization?
    a. A codified legal system
    b. Specialization of labor, and many people involved in nonfood production
    c. Monumental buildings
    d. A system for keeping permanent records

2. The peoples of ancient Mesopotamia tended to see the world as a hazardous place because
    a. their gods were inaccessible.
    b. the Tigris and Euphrates Rivers tended to flood unpredictably.
    c. of the constant warfare in their region.
    d. of the corruption of their government.

3. The successful operation of large-scale sophisticated irrigation systems generally depended on
   a. plentiful rainfall to justify such an expenditure of energy.
   b. the emergence of individuals or groups capable of compelling and organizing large numbers of people to work together.
   c. tremendous communal cooperation, usually led by local village councils.
   d. the importation of advanced technology and sometimes even of foreign workers.

4. How can scholars tell that protective city deities in Mesopotamia were important?
   a. the central locations of their temples.
   b. the wealth and power of their priests.
   c. extensive tracts of agricultural land the temples owned.
   d. their worship by surrounding peoples.

5. Many Mesopotamian states engaged in warfare mainly because
   a. they needed to gain access to raw materials through force.
   b. their religion demanded it.
   c. they constantly needed to defend their territory.
   d. they enjoyed it.

6. Why do we know so little about women in ancient Mesopotamia?
   a. Women were unimportant in Mesopotamian society.
   b. It was forbidden to discuss women in public.
   c. Male scribes tended to write about elite male activities.
   d. We know little about anyone in Mesopotamian society.

7. Which of the following best characterizes changes in women's status in the transition from hunting and gathering to agricultural societies?
   a. Women lost social standing and freedom.
   b. Women gained power and wealth.
   c. Women became less important in the public realm but more important in the sacred world.
   d. Women's status did not change.

8. For what purpose was writing developed?
   a. Economics
   b. History
   c. Law
   d. Astronomy

9. What commodity did Mesopotamia possess in abundance?
   a. Gold
   b. Silver
   c. Camels
   d. Clay

10. In Egypt, the ebb and flow of successful and failed regimes seem to be linked to
    a. trade.
    b. the cycle of floods.
    c. annual rainfall.
    d. the activity of surrounding peoples.

11. What single factor made construction of the pyramids possible?
    a. The wealth of the pharaohs
    b. Pulley technology
    c. Human muscle power
    d. Plentiful limestone

12. What circumstances led to Egypt becoming a focal point of civilization?
    a. outside conquest
    b. climatic change
    c. famine
    d. climatic change and famine

13. Why have the Indus stone seals *not* provided historians with a clear picture of Indus society?
    a. No one can read them.
    b. Indus peoples used riddles to confuse their enemies.
    c. The stone seals were not used for writing but for decoration.
    d. Indus peoples used stone seals only to write about people outside their own civilization.

14. Egypt's interests abroad focused primarily on
    a. conquest of territory
    b. acquisition of new slaves
    c. accumulating new technologies
    d. maintaining access to valuable resources

15. Why did Babylonians consider it necessary to annually restage the act of creation?
    a. It was part of the secular transfer of power to the new ruler.
    b. It was a celebration of thanksgiving for a good harvest.
    c. It ensured victory of life over death and restarted the cycle of time.
    d. It reaffirmed the superiority of the ruling class.

16. Indus society can best be described as
    a. urban
    b. rural
    c. imperial
    d. nomadic

Short-Answer Questions

Answer each question in one short paragraph, giving the definition, dates, and significance.

1. How can the term *civilization* be culturally biased?

2. Describe the ethnic makeup of the Mesopotamian region.

3. Discuss the role of the king in Mesopotamia. How much power did he have and what were his responsibilities?

4. How did Egypt's geography and climate influence religion and the outlook of the people? How did climatic events taking place from the fifth to the third millennium B.C.E. affect the growth of Egyptian civilization?

5. Compare and contrast the development of commerce in Mesopotamia and Egypt. Why did their styles differ?

6. Describe the process of mummification. Why was it done? Did burial techniques differ according to class?

7. Account for the differing status of women in Mesopotamian and Egyptian society.

8. If the writing left by the people of Indus is indecipherable, how do scholars know anything about them?

Essay Questions

Make an outline for each question, listing the major points you want to discuss. Then write your practice essay, following your outline carefully and making sure that you do not skip any of your major points. At this time you will want to add the relevant dates and details that will make your essay persuasive and accurate.

1. Discuss the Mesopotamian government structure. What could account for it? What are some of the advantages and disadvantages of this system?

2. Discuss the technology the Egyptians used for their monumental architecture. Who did the building and why?

3. Discuss some of the possible reasons for the decline and fall of the Indus civilization. Which theory or theories seem most plausible to historians and why?

4. Compare and contrast trade in the Mesopotamian, Egyptian, and Indus civilizations. How much trade was going on? How was it carried out and with whom? How important was it in each society?

5. Many historians believe that the world's first civilizations developed on the floodplains of large rivers. What other climatic conditions were usually present? How did the environment influence the growth of these civilizations?

Comparison Charts

Using information gathered from the text, fill in the blank areas of each chart with the relevant data pertaining to the regions and categories listed. (Not all blank areas will necessarily be used.)

Chart 2.1
ENVIRONMENT AND RELIGION

	Topography	Climate	Urban Geography	Government Structure	Social Structure	Laws	Religious Beliefs/Rituals	Cosmic Order	Attitude	Burial
Mesopotamia										
Egypt										

Chart 2.2
TECHNOLOGY

	Urban Planning	Agriculture and Irrigation	Mathe-matics	Science and Medicine	Uses of Metallurgy	Houses	Temples	Tombs	Transpor-tation	Writing	Calendars	Laws	Decorative Art
Mesopo-tamia													
Egypt													
Indus													

Society and Culture

After reading "Society and Culture: The Babylonian New Year's Festival" in your text, answer the following additional questions.

What is the significance of taking the scepter, circle, and sword from the king, and then returning them later? What was the role of the priest in the New Year's Festival? How powerful were the priests and why?

Internet Assignment

Keywords: **"Egyptian Hieroglyphics"**

"cuneiform"

"Indus seals"

Egyptian and Sumerian writings represent some of the earliest forms of writing in the ancient world. Try to imagine a world before writing—it's difficult for modern people because writing is so much a part of our world. But in ancient times, only a few people knew how to write, and writing had very specific uses. Use the above keywords to find web sites about ancient forms of writing. You might want to consult the *History WIRED* image library on the Bulliet, *The Earth and Its Peoples* web site (refer to the preface of this study guide for information on how to locate the Bulliet home page).

Who knew how to read and write in ancient societies? What was writing used for? How do the writing systems of Egypt, Sumeria, and the Indus differ? Where do scholars find ancient writings today, and what can they tell us about ancient worlds? What can we not learn from these writings and why?

Internet Exploration

When people think of the ancient Egyptians they think "mummies." Scholars too have benefited from the study of mummies and tombs. Look up the keywords "Egyptian mummification," and see what Egyptologists do every day.

Two specific sites you may like are ancienthistory.about.com/education/ancienthistory/library/howto/ht_mummy.htm?rnk=r&terms= mummies, and www.nationalgeographic.com/media/tv/mummy.

How difficult was the process of mummification? What does this tell us about death in ancient Egypt? Did mummification depend on social class? How do modern scholars study mummies, and what is done to preserve them?

Map Exercises

On Outline Map 2.1, shade in these ancient river civilizations:

Mesopotamia   China
Egypt   India

Then plot Jericho and Çatal Hüyük.

On Outline Map 2.2, mark the land of Mesopotamia. Then plot the following:

Tigris River   Sumer
Euphrates River   Uruk
Ashur   Babylon

On Outline Map 2.3, mark the region of Egypt. Then plot the following:

Nile River   Upper Nubia
Upper Egypt   Lower Nubia
Lower Egypt   Giza

Outline Map 2.1

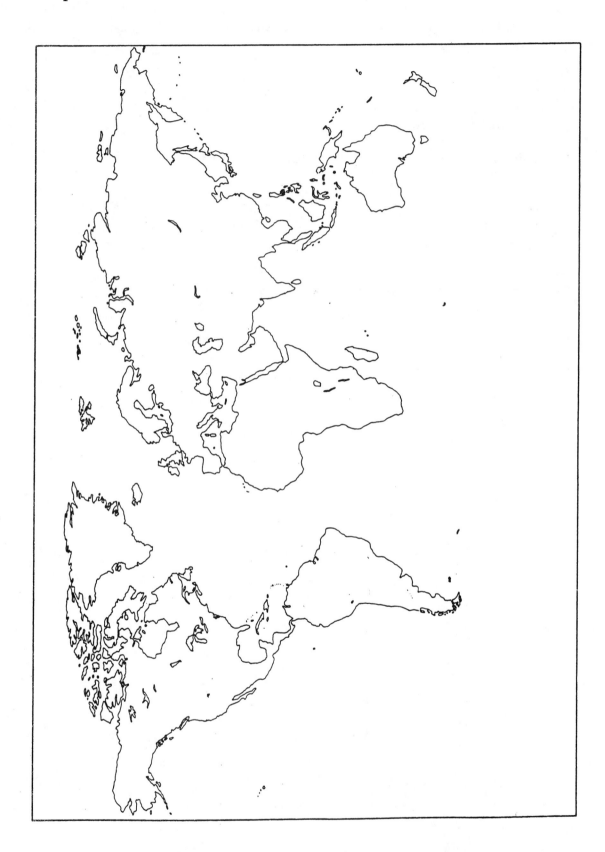

Outline Map 2.2

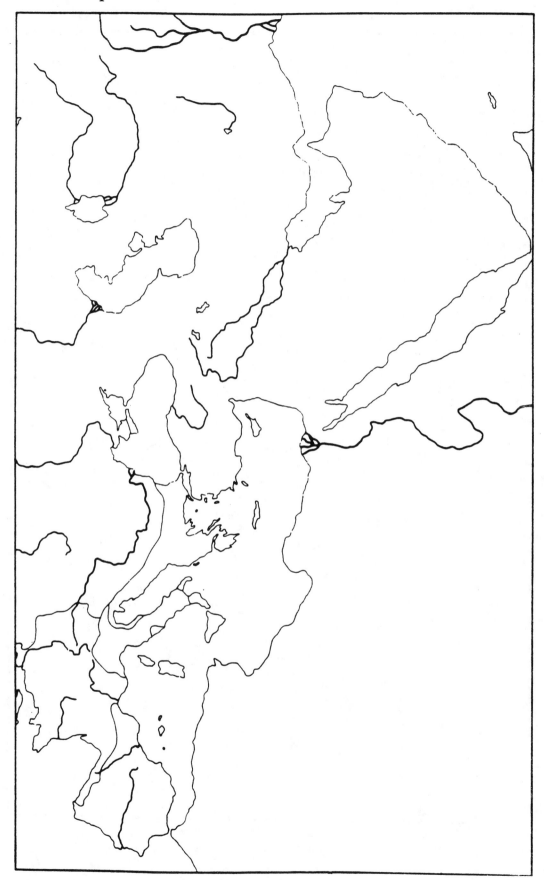

Outline Map 2.3

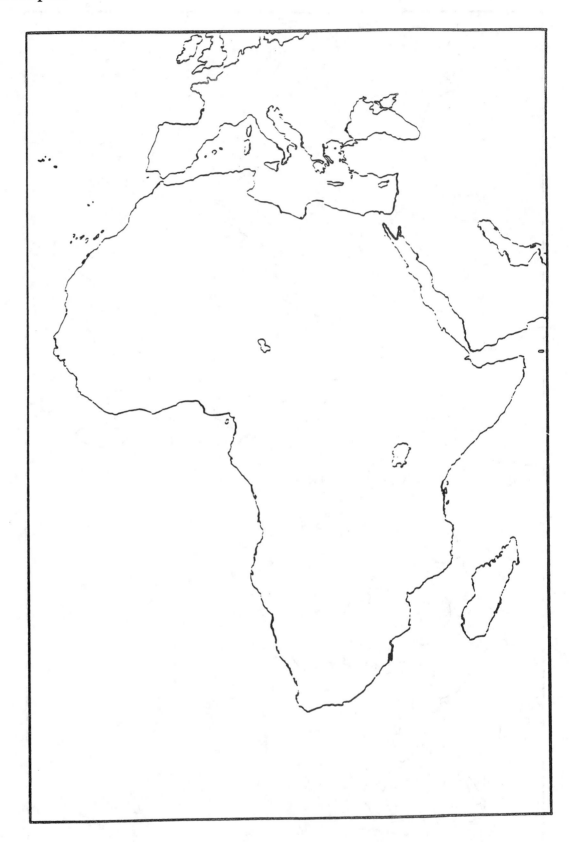

CHAPTER 3

The Late Bronze Age in the Eastern Hemisphere, 2200–500 B.C.E.

Learning Objectives

After reading Chapter 3 and completing this study chapter, you should be able to explain:

- Why western Eurasia saw the growth of many powerful states, which became linked through trade, politics, and warfare.

- How these states became interdependent and thus the failure of one could adversely affect those surrounding it.

- How early China developed independently of western Eurasia but still shared many of the same cultural attributes of the Mediterranean kingdoms, especially the use of bronze.

- What impact Egyptian culture had on Nubia, and how this region developed a culture that was influenced by Egypt and yet was distinctive.

- How environmental necessity mandated that the Greeks look toward the sea and trade for their livelihood, and what result this had.

Chapter Outline

In the outline below, include important themes, concepts, and details in the blank spaces provided. If you find fewer points than you have space for, leave lines blank. If you find more points, add as many lines as necessary.

I. Introduction

    A. *Queen Hatshepsut sent a naval expedition to Punt* _____

        1. _____

        2. _____

3. _____

B. *The major centers, such as the Nile civilization, pursue access to important resources* _____

  1. _____

  2. _____

  3. _____

C. *The movement of goods promoted the flow of ideas and technologies* _____

  1. _____

  2. _____

  3. _____

II. **Early China**

  A. *Geography and Resources* _____

   1. *Isolated from the rest of the Eastern Hemisphere* _____

    a. _____

    b. _____

    c. _____

   2. *Major geographical features* _____

    a. _____

    b. _____

    c. _____

    d. _____

    e. _____

   3. *The beginning of water control projects and results* _____

    a. _____

    b. _____

    c. _____

B.   *The Shang Period* _____

   1. *Neolithic Period and Xia dynasty* _____

      a. _____

      b. _____

      c. _____

   2. *Kings, administrators, warriors, and control* _____

      a. _____

      b. _____

      c. _____

      d. _____

      e. _____

      f. _____

   3. *Ideology of kingship and authority* _____

      a. _____

      b. _____

      c. _____

   4. *Other significant technological advances* _____

      a. _____

      b. _____

      c. _____

      d. _____

C.   *The Zhou Period* _____

1. *Keys to Zhou success* _____

    a. _____

    b. _____

    c. _____

2. *Western Zhou* _____

    a. _____

    b. _____

    c. _____

3. *Eastern Zhou* _____

    a. _____

    b. _____

    c. _____

4. *Confucianism* _____

    a. _____

    b. _____

    c. _____

    d. _____

    e. _____

    f. _____

5. *Women* _____

    a. _____

    b. _____

    c. _____

6. *Yin and yang* _____

    a. _____

    b. _____

    c. _____

III. **The Cosmopolitan Middle East**

  A. *Western Asia* _____

    1. *Babylonia in the south* _____

      a. _____

      b. _____

      c. _____

    2. *Assyria in the north* _____

      a. _____

      b. _____

      c. _____

    3. *Hittites* _____

      a. _____

      b. _____

      c. _____

    4. *Cultural diffusion* _____

      a. _____

      b. _____

      c. _____

  B. *New Kingdom Egypt* _____

    1. *For the first time Egypt under rule of non-Egyptians—Hyksos—Middle Kingdom*

   a. _____

   b. _____

   c. _____

2. *New Kingdom—native rulers return at Thebes* _____

   a. _____

   b. _____

   c. _____

3. *New Kingdom rulers* _____

   a. _____

   b. _____

   c. _____

C. *Commerce and Diplomacy* _____

1. *Syria-Palestine: negotiation and trade* _____

   a. _____

   b. _____

   c. _____

2. *Commerce in metals* _____

   a. _____

   b. _____

   c. _____

3. *New modes of transportation* _____

   a. _____

   b. _____

   c. _____

IV. **Nubia**

   A. *Early Cultures and Egyptian Domination*

      1. *Old Kingdom—relationship of trade*

         a. _____

         b. _____

         c. _____

      2. *Middle Kingdom—Egypt became more aggressive*

         a. _____

         b. _____

         c. _____

      3. *New Kingdom—Egypt pushed further into Nubia*

         a. _____

         b. _____

         c. _____

   B. *The Kingdom of Meroë*

      1. *Nubian rule of Egypt 712–660 B.C.E.*

         a. _____

         b. _____

         c. _____

      2. *By the 4th century B.C.E. power shifted south to Meroë*

         a. _____

         b. _____

         c. _____

3. *Royal women played important role in Meroë* _____

    a. _____

    b. _____

    c. _____

V. The Aegean World

A. *The Minoan Civilization of Crete* _____

  1. *Home of the first complex civilization in Europe* _____

    a. _____

    b. _____

    c. _____

  2. *Little is known about the Cretans—writing not translated—all knowledge from archaeology* _____

    a. _____

    b. _____

    c. _____

  3. *Evidence about women and religion* _____

    a. _____

    b. _____

    c. _____

B. *The Rise of Mycenaean Civilization* _____

  1. *First Greek civilization* _____

    a. _____

    b. _____

    c. _____

d. _____

2. *Evidence from shaft graves and clay tablets* _____

    a. _____

    b. _____

    c. _____

    d. _____

3. *Written sources contradictory* _____

    a. _____

    b. _____

    c. _____

C. *Overseas Commerce, Settlement, and Aggression* _____

1. *The role of seafaring* _____

    a. _____

    b. _____

    c. _____

2. *Exports* _____

    a. _____

    b. _____

    c. _____

3. *Imports* _____

    a. _____

    b. _____

    c. _____

4. *Pirates* _____

a. _____

b. _____

c. _____

VI.   The Fall of Late Bronze Age Civilizations

A.   *Migrations and invasions (subject heading not found in text)* _____

1. _____

a. _____

b. _____

c. _____

2. _____

a. _____

b. _____

c. _____

3. _____

a. _____

b. _____

c. _____

B.   *Fall of Mycenaean civilization (subject heading not found in text)* _____

1. _____

a. _____

b. _____

c. _____

2. _____

a. _____

    b. _____

    c. _____

  3. _____

    a. _____

    b. _____

    c. _____

C. *Aspects of civilization lost and retained (subject heading not found in text)*

  1. _____

    a. _____

    b. _____

    c. _____

  2. _____

    a. _____

    b. _____

    c. _____

  3. _____

    a. _____

    b. _____

    c. _____

VII. Conclusion

A. *Role of bronze metallurgy*

  1. _____

  2. _____

  3. _____

B. _____

    1. _____

    2. _____

    3. _____

C. *No fall in East Asia—why?* _____

    1. _____

    2. _____

    3. _____

Identifications

Define each term and explain why it is significant, including any important dates.

	Identification	*Significance*
loess		
Shang		
divination		
Zhou		
Son of Heaven		
Mandate of Heaven		
steppe nomads		
yin/yang		
Legalism		

	Identification	*Significance*
Confucius		
Daoism		
Hittites		
Hatshepsut		
Akhenaten		
Ramesses II		
Syria-Palestine		
camels		
Kush		
Meroë		
Minoan		
shaft grave		
fresco		
Linear B		
Mycenae		
Troy		
Amenhotep III		

Identification   *Significance*

bronze

oracle bones

Multiple-Choice Questions

Read the entire question, including *all* the possible answers. Then choose the *one* answer that best fits the question.

1. Shang authority was demonstrated by
    a. the happiness of the people.
    b. the size of urban centers.
    c. the possession of horses.
    d. the possession of cast bronze vessels for sacrifices to the gods.

2. Which of the following technologies was *not* developed by the end of the Shang dynasty?
    a. Monumental royal tombs
    b. The horse-drawn chariot
    c. Writing
    d. Gunpowder

3. In the Zhou period, the separation of religion from political dealings allowed China to
    a. make war on its neighbors.
    b. develop important secular philosophies.
    c. abandon all religious practices.
    d. adopt Buddhism.

4. Which of the following about the Eastern Zhou era is *not* true?
    a. It was a time of political fragmentation.
    b. Centers of power were shifting rapidly.
    c. Numerous small and independent states competed and warred with each other.
    d. The Xiongnu invaded Zhou lands.

5. How did the Egyptians' relationship with Nubia differ from their relationships with other territories they occupied?
    a. Nubia served as a buffer zone against invasion.
    b. They placed forts and garrisons of Egyptian soldiers in Nubia.
    c. They pressed the Nubian population to adopt Egyptian language and culture.
    d. The Egyptians extracted heavy tribute from the Nubians.

6. How did Egyptians respond to Hatshepsut's rule?
    a. They were opposed to the concept of having a woman as a ruler.
    b. They welcomed such an able ruler.
    c. They never knew she was a woman because drawings always showed her wearing a beard.
    d. They feared her because they thought she was a sorceress.

7. What was Akhenaten's motivation in modifying the Egyptian religion to emphasize the primacy of Aten (the sun)?
    a. He wanted to bring Egyptian religion more into line with other religions in the Middle East.
    b. He believed that worshiping the sun would increase agricultural production.
    c. He was attempting to reassert the superiority of the pharaoh and to renew belief in his own divinity.
    d. He hoped that by disillusioning the people he could make them abandon religion altogether and become better workers.

8. What was the source of the rivalry between Egypt and the Hittite kingdom?
    a. The question of who would rule the world
    b. Control of the trade routes in Syria-Palestine, the region lying between them
    c. Defining their mutual border
    d. The rich agricultural lands of Mesopotamia

9. The Nile's six cataracts
    a. did not affect trade in the slightest.
    b. required a combination of sailing and walking around the cataracts in order to trade.
    c. meant that trade in this region was by land only.
    d. completely discouraged trade.

10. Which of the following is *not* true about the rule of Nubian monarchs in Egypt?
    a. Nubian rule caused degeneration and decay in the arts and culture.
    b. The rulers were addressed by the traditional titles of Egyptian royalty.
    c. All subjects kept their Nubian names.
    d. The rulers were depicted in traditional costume and buried according to Egyptian custom.

11. Which of the following did *not* encourage the inhabitants of the Aegean islands to commence seafaring?
    a. Frequent flooding of their farmlands
    b. Scarcity of resources
    c. Natural harbors
    d. Rocky and arid land

12. What can scholars *not* prove about the relationship between the Minoans (Cretans) and the Mycenaeans?
    a. Cretan control of the mainland.
    b. Mycenaeans borrowed the idea of the palace, pottery, and writing.
    c. Mycenaeans borrowed the idea of centralized economy and administration.
    d. Greek culture is made of a mix of peoples from Crete and Mycenae.

13. The annihilation of the major trading partners and the disruption of trade routes
    a. helped bring about the end of Mycenaean civilization, thus illustrating the degree to which the major centers of the Late Bronze Age were interdependent.
    b. disrupted the Mycenaean economy in the short term.
    c. caused the merchants to demand equal voting rights.
    d. had no effect on the Mycenaean centers.

14. Why was China not affected by the fall of Bronze Age cultures in the rest of Eurasia?
    a. China was affected greatly by their fall.
    b. China was not dependent on bronze.
    c. The Chinese government was too strong.
    d. China was far away and not tightly linked by trade relations with the rest of Eurasia.

Short-Answer Questions

Answer each question in one short paragraph, giving the definition, dates, and significance.

1. Why did China develop independently from western Eurasia?

2. Discuss rice cultivation in China. How was rice grown, who did the work, and how did rice cultivation benefit the Chinese?

3. Describe the structure of the Zhou state.

4. Discuss the role and status of women in ancient China.

5. Discuss the shift in cultural patterns to sub-Saharan African models when Meroë became the focus of Nubian society.

6. Discuss how Egypt's New Kingdom differed from earlier eras in Egypt, particularly in its contact with the outside world.

7. Why did Akhenaten's reforms anger the priesthood?

Essay Questions

Make an outline for each question, listing the major points you want to discuss. Then write your practice essay, following your outline carefully and making sure that you do not skip any of your major points. At this time you will want to add the relevant dates and details that will make your essay persuasive and accurate.

1. Discuss the ideology of kingship during China's Shang dynasty. How did it compare with that of the Zhou dynasty?

2. Discuss the Hyksos' control of Egypt and the Egyptian response. How was the New Kingdom inaugurated? What were its major challenges and achievements?

3. Describe the rise of Nubia and its relationship with Egypt. Why was Nubia attracted to Egypt? What did it gain?

4. Discuss the fall of Mycenae. How was it related to other events in the region?

5. Compare and contrast the different philosophical systems of the Zhou dynasty.

Comparison Charts

Using information gathered from the text, fill in the blank areas of each chart with the relevant data pertaining to the regions and categories listed. (Not all blank areas will necessarily be used.)

Chart 3.1
BRONZE AND ITS USES

	Date They Developed Bronze Technology	Where Did They Get the Technology	Where Did They Get the Ore	Control of Bronze	Coinage	Ritual Implements	Tools	Weapons	Other
Chinese									
Assyrians									
Egyptians									
Nubians									
Early Greeks									

Chart 3.2
NUBIA AND THE AEGEAN WORLD

Region	Geography	Dates	Type of Government	Social System	Religion	Outside Influences	Trade/ Economy	Technology
Nubia								
Aegean World								

Society and Culture

After reading "Society and Culture: The Amarna Letters" in your text, answer the following additional questions.

Do you think the humble salutations used by the subject kings of Egypt accurately reflect their view of themselves? How might they have felt about their Egyptian overlords, and what evidence of this do you find in the Amarna Letters?

Internet Assignment

Keywords: "oracle bones"

                "Mask of Agamemnon" or "Mycenaean mask"

The oracle bones date from Shang dynasty China, and the Mask of Agamemnon dates from Mycenaean Greece. Both of these artifacts were found within the last one hundred and fifty years. Their discovery taught scholars something important that was unproven at the time of their unearthing. Use the above keywords to find web sites about these artifacts. You might want to consult the *History WIRED* image library on the Bulliet, *The Earth and Its Peoples* website (refer to the preface of this study guide for information on how to locate the Bulliet home page). What did we learn from these pieces of evidence? What can't these artifacts prove?

Internet Exploration

Go to Egypt this weekend! Visit some of Egypt's breathtaking monuments online; miss out on the camels, the dust, and the airfare. Two wonderful monuments available are Ramses II's temple and the tomb of Tutankhamun. One site you may enjoy is <u>Nova Online Adventure</u> for an interactive tour featuring many of the sights of ancient Egypt: <u>www.pbs.org/wgbh/nova/egypt/textindex.html</u>.

You might also try the keywords "Ramses II temple" or "Tutankhamun."

Map Exercises

On Outline Map 3.1, mark the extent of the Shang dynasty and the Zhou dynasty. Also, trace the winter monsoon winds and summer monsoon winds.

On Outline Map 3.2, shade in the Hittite Empire; the area dominated by Mesopotamian culture; and the area dominated by Egyptian culture.

On Outline Map 3.3, shade in Minoan Greece and Mycenaean Greece. Then label the following:

Corinth   Crete
Attica   Thrace
Peloponnese   Messenia

Cnossus

On Outline Map 3.4, shade in ancient Nubia and label the following:

The six cataracts	Thebes
Meroë	Aswan
Kush	
Memphis	

Outline Map 3.1

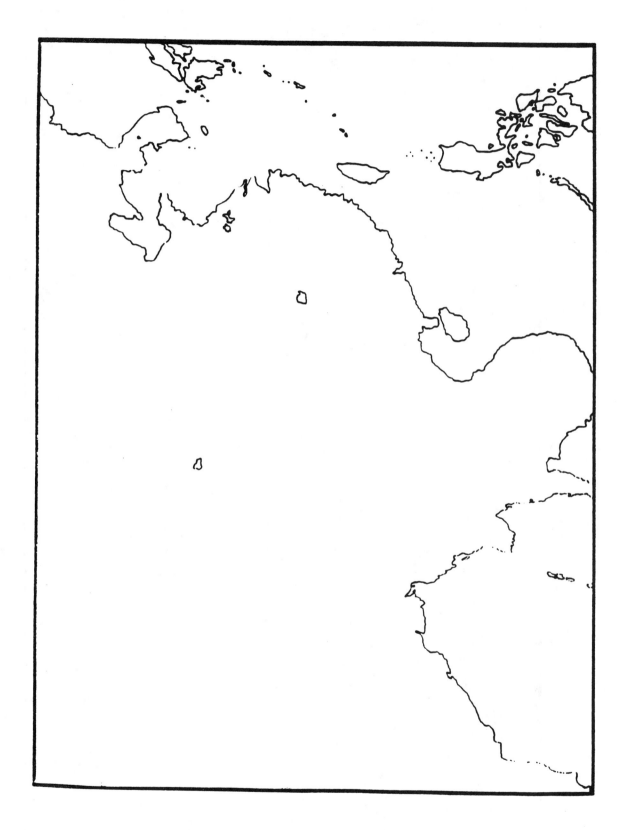

Outline Map 3.2

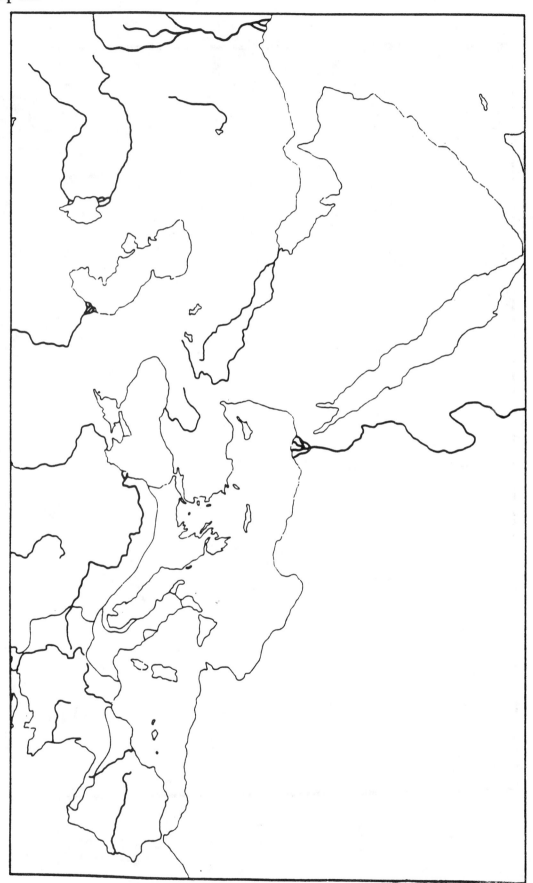

Outline Map 3.3

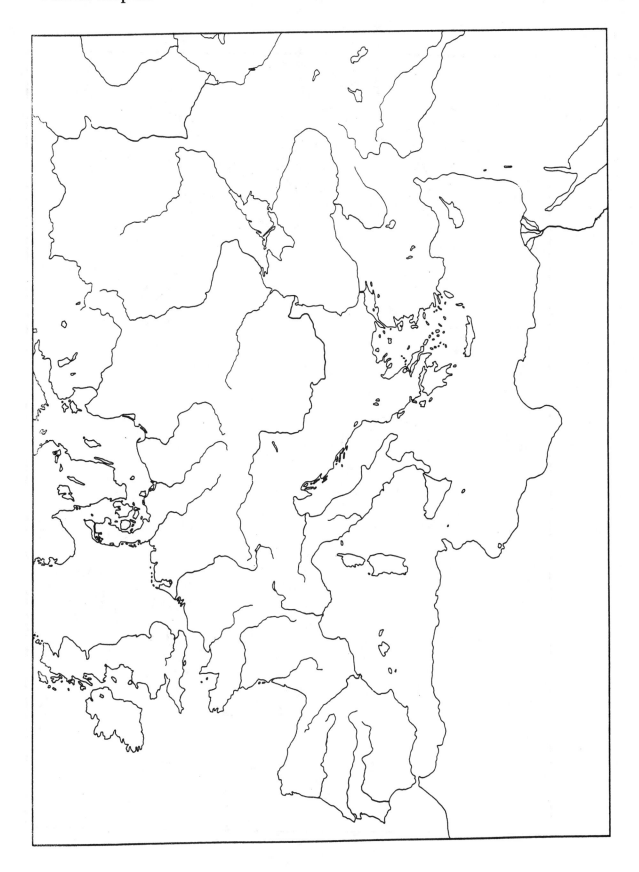

Outline Map 3.4

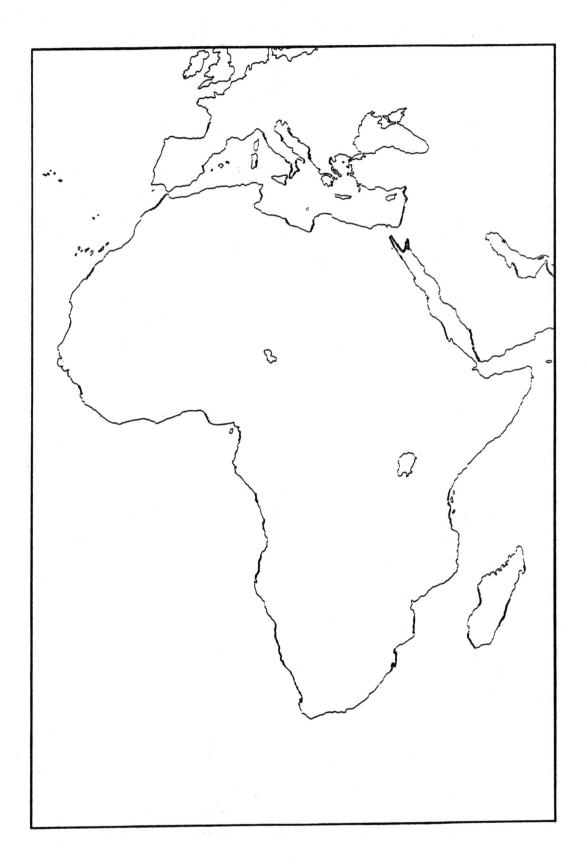

CHAPTER 4

New Civilizations in the Americas and Western Eurasia, 1200–250 B.C.E.

Learning Objectives

After reading Chapter 4 and completing this study chapter, you should be able to explain:

- How the environment may have influenced the development of the peoples of the Western and Eastern Hemisphere.

- What motivated the migrations of the Celts and the Israelites, and how their cultures survived despite their conquest by empires.

- How the early Iron Age was a time of migration of large numbers of people, and what impact those migrations had on the land and peoples of that period.

- How land-based and sea-based empires differed from each other in style, technique, and philosophical outlook.

- What new complex political, social, and economic structures evolved in the era of empire building.

Chapter Outline

In the outline below, include important themes, concepts, and details in the blank spaces provided. If you find fewer points than you have space for, leave lines blank. If you find more points, add as many lines as necessary.

I. **Introduction**

    A. *Dido and the founding of Carthage* _____

        1. _____

        2. _____

3. _____

B. *Migration and resettlement in the Mediterranean region and western Asia* _____

1. _____

2. _____

3. _____

C. *The rise of complex societies in the Western Hemisphere* _____

1. _____

2. _____

3. _____

II. **First Civilizations of the Americas**

A. *The Mesoamerican Olmecs, 1200–400 B.C.E.* _____

1. *Three Olmec centers* _____

a. _____

b. _____

c. _____

2. *Agriculture* _____

a. _____

b. _____

c. _____

3. *Urban development and mass labor* _____

a. _____

b. _____

c. _____

　　d. _____

　　e. _____

4.　*Politics* _____

　　a. _____

　　b. _____

　　c. _____

5.　*Trade and influence* _____

　　a. _____

　　b. _____

　　c. _____

　　d. _____

　　e. _____

　　f. _____

6.　*Religion* _____

　　a. _____

　　b. _____

　　c. _____

B.　*Early South American Civilization: Chavín 900–250* B.C.E. _____

　1.　*Geography and Chavín Huantar* _____

　　a. _____

　　b. _____

　　c. _____

　　d. _____

　2.　*Chavín's political and cultural dominance* _____

a. _____

b. _____

c. _____

3. *Agriculture, labor, and trade* _____

   a. _____

   b. _____

   c. _____

   d. _____

   e. _____

   f. _____

4. *Metallurgy and textiles* _____

   a. _____

   b. _____

   c. _____

5. *Class distinctions* _____

   a. _____

   b. _____

   c. _____

III. Celtic Europe

A. *The Spread of the Celts* _____

   1. *Celtic linguistic designation linked with Celtic culture* ___

     a. _____

     b. _____

    c. _____

2. *Rapid expansion of Celtic groups in several directions*

    a. _____

    b. _____

    c. _____

3. *Greek and Roman views of Celtic appearance*

    a. _____

    b. _____

    c. _____

B. *Celtic Society*

1. *Celtic classes*

    a. _____

    b. _____

    c. _____

2. *Celtic priests—Druids*

    a. _____

    b. _____

    c. _____

    d. _____

    e. _____

3. *Agriculture and shipbuilding*

    a. _____

    b. _____

    c. _____

4. *Celtic women* _____

    a. _____

    b. _____

    c. _____

    d. _____

    e. _____

    f. _____

C. *Belief and Knowledge* _____

  1. *Deities and worship* _____

    a. _____

    b. _____

    c. _____

  2. *Burial and other worlds* _____

    a. _____

    b. _____

    c. _____

  3. *Roman conquest* _____

    a. _____

    b. _____

    c. _____

III. The Assyrian Empire

A. *God and King* _____

  1. *Symbolism of kingship* _____

    a. _____

    b. _____

    c. _____

2.   *Duties of the king* _____

    a. _____

    b. _____

    c. _____

    d. _____

    e. _____

    f. _____

3.   *Government propaganda* _____

    a. _____

    b. _____

    c. _____

B. *Conquest and control* _____

    1.   *Military technology a fundamental factor of success* _____

        a. _____

        b. _____

        c. _____

        d. _____

        e. _____

        f. _____

    2.   *Terror tactics discouraged resistance and rebellion* _____

        a. _____

b. _____

c. _____

d. _____

e. _____

f. _____

3. *Challenges to organization and communication* _____

   a. _____

   b. _____

   c. _____

   d. _____

   e. _____

   f. _____

4. *Administration* _____

   a. _____

   b. _____

   c. _____

   d. _____

   e. _____

   f. _____

5. *Exploitation of wealth and people* _____

   a. _____

   b. _____

   c. _____

d. _____

e. _____

C. *Assyrian Society and Culture* _____

   1. *Four classes in Assyrian society* _____

      a. _____

      b. _____

      c. _____

      d. _____

   2. *All free people had some legal protections* _____

      a. _____

      b. _____

      c. _____

   3. *Agriculture and artisans* _____

      a. _____

      b. _____

      c. _____

   4. *Continuing scientific developments* _____

      a. _____

      b. _____

      c. _____

      d. _____

      e. _____

   5. *Libraries* _____

      a. _____

b. _____

c. _____

IV. Israel

A. *Origins, Exodus, and Settlement* _____

1. *The Hebrew Bible as a historical source* _____

   a. _____

   b. _____

   c. _____

   d. _____

   e. _____

   f. _____

2. *Story of nomadic pastoralists* _____

   a. _____

   b. _____

   c. _____

3. *The experiences of Abraham may encompass the experiences of generations* ___

   a. _____

   b. _____

   c. _____

   d. _____

   e. _____

   f. _____

   g. _____

4. *Israelite slaves and the Exodus* _____

a. _____

b. _____

c. _____

d. _____

e. _____

f. _____

5. *The conquest of Canaan and forging a coalition* _____

   a. _____

   b. _____

   c. _____

B. *Rise of the monarchy* _____

1. *The Philistines and Saul the first king of Israel* _____

   a. _____

   b. _____

   c. _____

2. *David* _____

   a. _____

   b. _____

   c. _____

   d. _____

   e. _____

3. *Solomon and the First Temple* _____

   a. _____

b. _____

c. _____

d. _____

e. _____

4.   *Family and women* _____

a. _____

b. _____

c. _____

d. _____

e. _____

f. _____

C.   *Fragmentation and Dispersal* _____

1.   *The division into Israel and Judea and resulting invasions* _____

a. _____

b. _____

c. _____

d. _____

e. _____

f. _____

2.   *The Diaspora and Babylonian Jews* _____

a. _____

b. _____

c. _____

d. _____

e. _____

3. *The Deuteronomic Code and Jewish cohesion* _____

   a. _____

   b. _____

   c. _____

   d. _____

   e. _____

V. **Phoenicia and the Mediterranean**

A. *The Phoenician City-States* _____

   1. *Geography and the early Phoenician state* _____

      a. _____

      b. _____

      c. _____

   2. *Phoenicians first to develop an alphabetic system* _____

      a. _____

      b. _____

      c. _____

   3. *Byblos* _____

      a. _____

      b. _____

      c. _____

   4. *Tyre* _____

      a. _____

      b. _____

      c. _____

      d. _____

      e. _____

B. *Expansion into the Mediterranean* _____

  1. *The formation of the Phoenician triangle* _____

      a. _____

      b. _____

      c. _____

      d. _____

  2. *The necessity for expansion* _____

      a. _____

      b. _____

      c. _____

  3. *Conflicts with the Greeks over Sicily* _____

      a. _____

      b. _____

      c. _____

C. *Carthage's Commercial Empire* _____

  1. *Founding of Carthage and its strategic elements* _____

      a. _____

      b. _____

      c. _____

      d. _____

e. _____

f. _____

2. *The design of the city itself and population* _____

   a. _____

   b. _____

   c. _____

3. *Administration and rule by merchant Senate* _____

   a. _____

   b. _____

   c. _____

4. *Navy, ship design, and foreign policy* _____

   a. _____

   b. _____

   c. _____

   d. _____

   e. _____

D. *War and Religion*

1. *Carthage: a different kind of empire* _____

   a. _____

   b. _____

   c. _____

2. *The importance of civilians and the resulting approach to the military and war*

   a. _____

   b. _____

c. _____

d. _____

3. *Religion and child sacrifice* _____

a. _____

b. _____

c. _____

VI. **Failure and Transformation**

A. *Assyrian role in the events of the region* _____

1. _____

2. _____

3. _____

4. _____

5. _____

B. *First cause of Assyrian decline was the resurgence of Babylon* _____

1. _____

2. _____

3. _____

C. *Second reason for Assyrian decline was invasion by the Medes* _____

1. _____

2. _____

3. _____

VII. **Conclusion**

A. *Success and growth of human populations in Eastern Hemisphere may be due to environment*

1. _____

   2. _____

   3. _____

B. *Environment may have inhibited development in the Americas* _____

   1. _____

   2. _____

   3. _____

C. *Population movement* _____

   1. _____

   2. _____

   3. _____

   4. _____

   5. _____

Identifications

Define each term and explain why it is significant, including any important dates.

	Identification	*Significance*
Olmec		
Chavín		
llama		
Jaguar symbol		
Iron Age		
Celts		

	Identification	*Significance*
Druids		
Neo-Assyrian Empire		
Ashur		
mass deportation		
Library of Ashurbanipal		
Hebrew Bible		
Temple		
monotheism		
Diaspora		
Phoenicians		
Carthage		
murex snail		
Phoenician triangle		
Sicily		
Senate		
tophet		
Neo-Babylonian kingdom		

Multiple-Choice Questions

Read the entire question, including *all* the possible answers. Then choose the *one* answer that best fits the question.

1. Most scholars think that the American continents have
   a. had some contact with other continents over the last ten thousand years.
   b. been virtually isolated from the rest of the world for the last fifteen thousand years.
   c. been frequently visited by peoples from Asia.
   d. been frequently visited by peoples from Africa.

2. Mesoamerica was never united
   a. politically.
   b. economically.
   c. religiously.
   d. culturally.

3. The Olmecs can be described as
   a. ruling over a great empire.
   b. a great military power.
   c. the first civilization of Peru.
   d. never having an empire, but influencing regions by controlling commodities such as jade.

4. Why did the Celtic peoples enter the historical record?
   a. They became advanced enough to be considered a legitimate society.
   b. They came in contact with the literate peoples of the Mediterranean.
   c. They developed writing.
   d. They won the war against the Macedonians.

5. The Romans eliminated the Druids because they
   a. would not convert to Roman Catholicism.
   b. would not reveal their mystical knowledge.
   c. caused divisiveness within Celtic society.
   d. could have served as a rallying point for Celtic opposition.

6. Which of the following is *not* a way in which Celtic women differed from their Middle Eastern or Greek and Roman counterparts?
   a. Celtic women participated equally with men in warfare.
   b. Celtic women occasionally served as queens of their tribes.
   c. Celtic women had greater sexual freedom.
   d. Celtic women had the right to inherit the family estate.

7. Which was the first real empire in world history?
   a. Mesopotamia
   b. Egypt
   c. Assyria
   d. China

8. Why did the rulers of the Neo-Assyrian military follow the trade routes in their campaigns?
   a. The caravans were an excellent source of booty.
   b. The roads were good.
   c. They could disguise themselves as traders.
   d. By controlling the trade routes, they blocked all entry into Assyria.

9. What made possible the Assyrians' conquest of their empire?
    a. Their tolerance for the desires of their subjects
    b. Their military organization and technology
    c. Their superior manufacturing and trade networks
    d. Their religious system for legitimating rule

10. In Assyria, the term *human beings* referred to
    a. all people of the empire.
    b. ethnic Assyrians only.
    c. military and civil elites only.
    d. all peoples of the world.

11. The text of the Hebrew Bible (Old Testament) best reflects the view of
    a. the fifth century B.C.E. priests who controlled the Temple of Jerusalem.
    b. the twelve apostles.
    c. the prophet Abraham.
    d. the medieval Christian monks who compiled both the Old and New Testaments from the Hebrew and Greek texts.

12. Because of its lack of land, the Phoenician civilization concentrated on
    a. waging wars to acquire more land.
    b. religious pursuits.
    c. trade and manufacturing.
    d. hiring themselves out as mercenaries.

13. Who developed the first alphabetic system of writing?
    a. Phoenicians
    b. Greeks
    c. Canaanites
    d. Mesopotamians

14. Why do historians know more about Carthage than they know about the Phoenician homeland?
    a. The Phoenicians developed writing only after establishing Carthage.
    b. Roman and Greek records tell more about Carthage than other Phoenician city-states.
    c. When the Persians took over the eastern Mediterranean, they burned all the old Phoenician records.
    d. Carthage was simply more important throughout time than any other Phoenician city.

15. Textile production has generally been the preserve of women because
    a. it was easy and undemanding.
    b. it was possible to care for children and spin or weave at the same time.
    c. men's hands are too large and clumsy to work with textiles.
    d. women are more fashion conscious.

16. How many murex snails does it take to produce one gram of purple dye?
    a. One
    b. Thirty
    c. Five hundred
    d. Nine thousand

Short-Answer Questions

Answer each question in one short paragraph, giving the definition, dates, and significance.

1. What was the impact of the llama on Chavín culture?

2. To what geographical regions did the Celts spread? Why? How were they received?

3. Describe the responsibilities of the Assyrian kings. What were their methods? How successful were they?

4. How did the Assyrians use propaganda? How effective was it?

5. Discuss the repercussions of the Diaspora.

6. Discuss the rules followed by Jews. How have they helped and/or hindered Jews?

7. Characterize the relationship between Solomon and Hiram. How did they help each other?

Essay Questions

Make an outline for each question, listing the major points you want to discuss. Then write your practice essay, following your outline carefully and making sure that you do not skip any of your major points. At this time you will want to add the relevant dates and details that will make your essay persuasive and accurate.

1. What are the causes, means, and consequences of large-scale migrations of people? Use examples from at least three peoples.

2. Why is the Assyrian Empire considered to be the first in the world? What were its attributes and legacies?

3. Discuss the use of the Bible as a historical source. What are the advantages and disadvantages of such use for the scholar? Compare and contrast some of the biblical interpretations with those suggested by some modern historians.

4. Compare and contrast the rise of the civilizations of the Celts, Assyria, Israel, and the Americas. What were their goals and methods?

5. How did Phoenicia differ from the civilizations of the Celts, Assyria, Israel, and the Americas?

6. Discuss the legacies of the Olmec and Chavín cultures. What aspects of their cultures survived to influence later peoples?

Comparison Charts

Using information gathered from the text, fill in the blank areas of each chart with the relevant data pertaining to the regions and categories listed. (Not all blank areas will necessarily be used.)

Chart 4.1
MIGRATIONS

	When	Original Homeland	Destination	Why	Livelihood	Method of Migration	Response of Native Peoples
Celts							
Israelites							
Phoenicians							

Chart 4.2
TWO EMPIRES

Regions	Government System	Military Technology	Nonmilitary Technology	Economy	Society	Status of Women	Role of Civilians
Assyria							
Phoenicia							

Society and Culture

After reading "Society and Culture: Mass Deportation in the Neo-Assyrian Empire" in your text, answer the following additional questions.

When King Sargon II defeated Samaria he only removed a portion of the population, maintaining social structure and occupations for the remaining citizens. Why would he disrupt Samarian society so much, and then try to reinstate normality? How would this benefit the Assyrian state? How would those left behind in Samaria adjust to their new lives? What challenges would they face with the loss of their elite members and artisans?

Internet Assignment

Keywords: "megaliths"

                "Olmec heads"

The European megaliths, like Stonehenge, and the Olmec heads are two examples of large stone works. Use the above keywords to find web sites about European megaliths and Olmec heads. You might want to consult the *History WIRED* image library on the Bulliet, *The Earth and Its Peoples* web site (refer to the preface of this study guide for information on how to locate Bulliet home page).

How do they differ in appearance and use in society? How were they made and transported? Explore the various theories. Which theories seem the most reasonable?

Internet Exploration

Underwater archaeology is a growing, exciting field, and new discoveries are made each year. Recently archaeologists have found a number of sunken Phoenician ships. This is particularly helpful as we know little about the Phoenicians. Use the keywords "Phoenician shipwrecks" to learn more about what the Phoenicians shipped, and the controversy surrounding their identity.

Map Exercises

On Outline Map 4.1, shade in the regions where the following occurred:

Early Celtic settlement
Celtic diffusion by 500 B.C.E.

Celtic diffusion by 300 B.C.E.
Celtic diffusion by 200 B.C.E.

Then plot Britain and Rome.

On Outline Map 4.2, shade in these areas:

Assyrian Empire
Phoenicia
Israel

Judah
Egypt

Then plot Babylon, Galilee, and Canaan.

On Outline Map 4.3, shade in these areas:

The extent of the Olmec civilization

The extent of the Chavín civilization

Outline Map 4.1

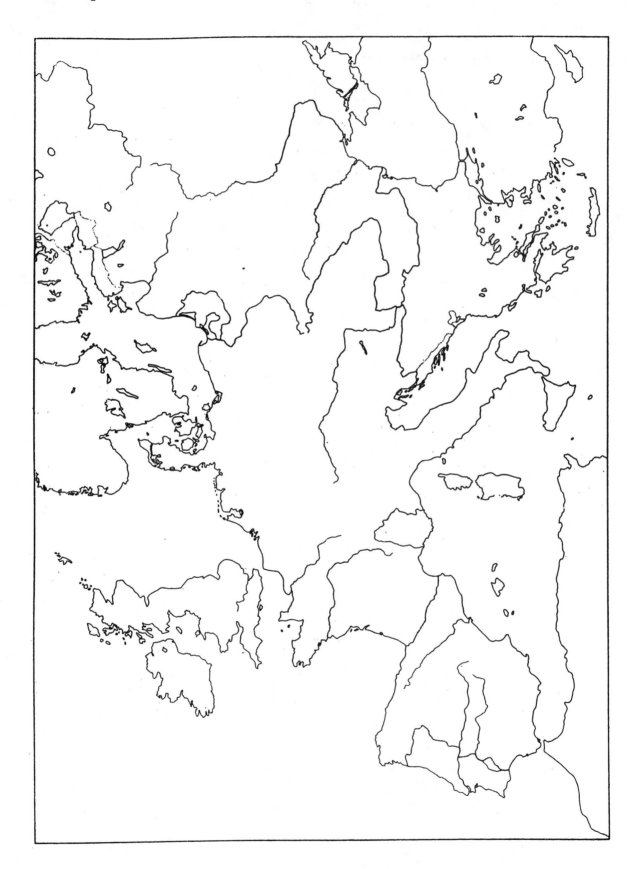

Outline Map 4.2

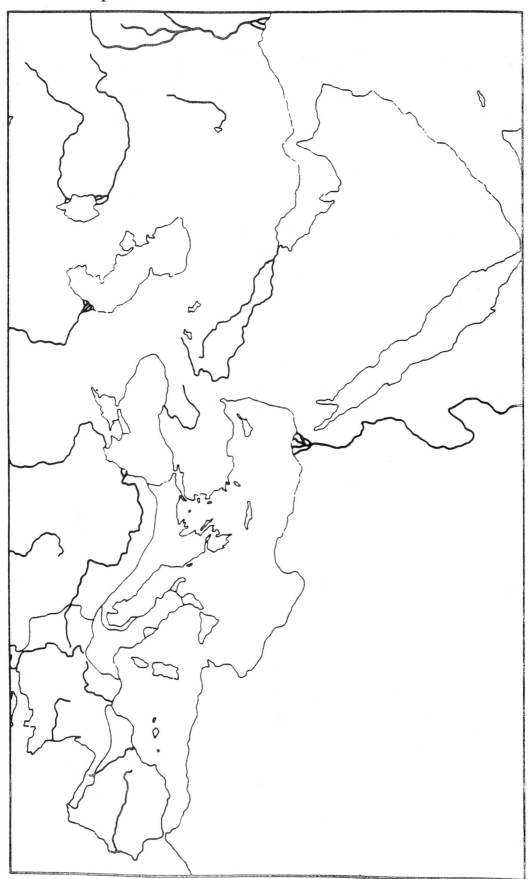

Outline Map 4.3

CHAPTER 5
Greece and Iran, 1000–30 B.C.E.

Learning Objectives

After reading Chapter 5 and completing this study chapter, you should be able to explain:

- How ancient Iran functioned as a link between western Asia and southern and Central Asia, and how its history has been influenced by this role.

- How Persia rose from nomadic roots to become the largest land empire the world had ever seen, both with original innovations and borrowed culture from its Mesopotamian predecessors.

- In what ways the environment of the Mediterranean region offered both opportunities and limited choices for its inhabitants.

- How Greek civilization developed and evolved into a sophisticated culture, often marred by competition between the various Greek city-states.

- What characterized the relationship between the Persians and the Greeks, and how much they had in common despite being rivals.

Chapter Outline

In the outline below, include important themes, concepts, and details in the blank spaces provided. If you find fewer points than you have space for, leave lines blank. If you find more points, add as many lines as necessary.

I. Introduction

    A. *All people view their own customs as natural and culturally superior*

        1. _____

        2. _____

3. _____

B. *The Persian Empire brought diverse peoples together* _____

   1. _____

   2. _____

   3. _____

C. *Beginnings of east-west conflict* _____

   1. _____

   2. _____

   3. _____

II. Ancient Iran

A. *Geography and Resources* _____

   1. *Harsh conditions—limited water resources* _____

      a. _____

      b. _____

      c. _____

   2. *Developed irrigation in first millennium B.C.E.* _____

      a. _____

      b. _____

      c. _____

   3. *Mineral resources exploited minimally* _____

      a. _____

      b. _____

      c. _____

B. *The Rise of the First Persian Empire* _____

   1. *Migration and conquest* _____

      a. _____

      b. _____

      c. _____

   2. *Shift in power from Medes to Persians and patrilineal society* _____

      a. _____

      b. _____

      c. _____

   3. *The rule of Cyrus* _____

      a. _____

      b. _____

      c. _____

      d. _____

   4. *Cambyses and Darius* _____

      a. _____

      b. _____

      c. _____

C. *Imperial Organization and Ideology* _____

   1. *Empire divided into twenty provinces, each led by a satrap* _____

      a. _____

      b. _____

      c. _____

      d. _____

2. *The royal family* _____

    a. _____

    b. _____

    c. _____

    d. _____

3. *Administration of empire* _____

    a. _____

    b. _____

    c. _____

    d. _____

    e. _____

3. *Connection between Zoroastrianism and Persian rule* _____

    a. _____

    b. _____

    c. _____

III. The Rise of the Greeks

A. *Geography and Resources* _____

1. *The Mediterranean* _____

    a. _____

    b. _____

    c. _____

2. *The Aegean Sea, islands and rivers* _____

    a. _____

b. _____

c. _____

3. *Factors that drew the Greeks to the sea* _____

    a. _____

    b. _____

    c. _____

B. *The Emergence of the Polis* _____

1. *The "Dark Ages" and the Phoenicians* _____

    a. _____

    b. _____

    c. _____

    d. _____

2. *The alphabet* _____

    a. _____

    b. _____

    c. _____

3. *Society, urban centers, and warfare* _____

    a. _____

    b. _____

    c. _____

    d. _____

    e. _____

4. *Colonies and Greek culture* _____

    a. _____

b. _____

c. _____

d. _____

e. _____

5. *From tyrants to oligarchy or democracy* _____

   a. _____

   b. _____

   c. _____

   d. _____

6. *Religion* _____

   a. _____

   b. _____

   c. _____

C. *New Intellectual Currents* _____

1. *Growing interest in the individual* _____

   a. _____

   b. _____

   c. _____

2. *Challenges to traditional religion* _____

   a. _____

   b. _____

   c. _____

   d. _____

3. *Historia* _____

    a. _____

    b. _____

    c. _____

D. *Athens and Sparta* _____

1. *Sparta* _____

    a. _____

    b. _____

    c. _____

    d. _____

    e. _____

2. *Athens* _____

    a. _____

    b. _____

    c. _____

    d. _____

    e. _____

3. *Democracy* _____

    a. _____

    b. _____

    c. _____

IV. **The Struggle of Persia and Greece**

A. *Early encounters* _____

1. *The Ionian Revolt* _____

    a. _____

    b. _____

    c. _____

2.   *The Persian Wars* _____

    a. _____

    b. _____

    c. _____

3.   *The Hellenic League* _____

    a. _____

    b. _____

    c. _____

4.   *Greeks attack Persia and the formation of the Delian League* _____

    a. _____

    b. _____

    c. _____

B.   *The Height of Athenian Power* _____

1.   *Path to power* _____

    a. _____

    b. _____

    c. _____

2.   *Navy* _____

    a. _____

    b. _____

c. _____

d. _____

e. _____

3. *Political power and commercial interests* _____

   a. _____

   b. _____

   c. _____

4. *Socrates* _____

   a. _____

   b. _____

   c. _____

C. *Inequality in Classical Greece* _____

   1. *Who benefited from democracy?* _____

      a. _____

      b. _____

      c. _____

   2. *Slavery* _____

      a. _____

      b. _____

      c. _____

   3. *Women and marriage* _____

      a. _____

      b. _____

      c. _____

        d. _____

        e. _____

D. *Failure of the City-State and Triumph of the Macedonians* _____

    1.   *The Peloponnesian War* _____

        a. _____

        b. _____

        c. _____

        d. _____

    2.   *Triumph of Macedonia* _____

        a. _____

        b. _____

        c. _____

    3.   *Alexander's methods of rule* _____

        a. _____

        b. _____

        c. _____

V. The Hellenistic Synthesis

    A. *Changes after the death of Alexander (this subject heading does not appear in text)* ___

        1. _____

        a. _____

        b. _____

        c. _____

        2.   *Seleucid rule* _____

a. _____

b. _____

c. _____

3.   *Ptolemic rule* _____

    a. _____

    b. _____

    c. _____

    d. _____

4.   *Antigonid dynasty* _____

    a. _____

    b. _____

    c. _____

B.   *Athens and Sparta (this subject heading does not appear in text)* _____

1.   *Stood out from these federations* _____

    a. _____

    b. _____

    c. _____

2.   *Alexandria* _____

    a. _____

    b. _____

    c. _____

3.   *Benefits of citizenship* _____

    a. _____

    b. _____

c. _____

C. *The Hellenistic states (this subject heading does not appear in text)* _____

   1. *Indigenous population* _____

      a. _____

      b. _____

      c. _____

   2. *New wisdom* _____

      a. _____

      b. _____

      c. _____

   3. *New cultural and religious practices* _____

      a. _____

      b. _____

      c. _____

VI. Conclusion

A. *Profound changes—Persians and Greeks play pivotal roles* _____

   1. _____

   2. _____

   3. _____

B. *Persian supremacy* _____

   1. _____

   2. _____

   3. _____

   4. _____

5. _____

6. _____

C. *Alexander and Hellenism* _____

    1. _____

    2. _____

    3. _____

Identifications

Define each term and explain why it is significant, including any important dates.

	Identification	*Significance*
Cyrus (Kurush)		
Darius (Darayavaush)		
satrap		
Susa		
Persepolis (Parsa)		
Zoroastrianism		
polis		
Athens		
Sparta		
hoplite		
tyrant		

Identification *Significance*

democracy

humanism

sacrifice

Herodotus

Plato

Pericles

Persian Wars

trireme

Socrates

Peloponnesian War

Alexander

Hellenistic Age

Ptolemies

Alexandria

Multiple-Choice Questions

Read the entire question, including *all* the possible answers. Then choose the *one* answer that best fits the question.

1. The geographic location of Iran (ancient Persia)
   a. makes it a formidable barrier between east and west.
   b. makes it a link between West, South, and Central Asia.
   c. indicates that the major trading routes, such as the Silk Road, did not pass through it.
   d. indicates that the region received plenty of monsoonal rainfall, eliminating the need for large-scale irrigation.

2. Which of the following statements best characterizes the differences between the Medes and the Persians?
   a. They formed two distinct ethnic groups, speaking mutually unintelligible dialects.
   b. There was no difference between them as both names refer to the same people.
   c. They were often at odds with each other throughout Iran's history.
   d. They were so similar that the Greeks could not tell them apart.

3. Why did Cyrus prevail at the battle of Sardis, the capital of Lydia (in Anatolia)?
   a. He conspired with the disgruntled inhabitants of the city to throw open the gates to his army.
   b. He used the newly invented catapult to break down the city walls.
   c. The smell of his camels disconcerted the enemy's horses.
   d. Cyrus lost the battle of Sardis in 546 B.C.E.

4. Why did satrapies have more autonomy the farther they were from the central seat of government?
   a. Communication was so slow that it was impractical to refer matters to the central government.
   b. Outlying areas were constantly beguiled by neighboring peoples to follow their own course.
   c. Outlying areas were too hard to defend from invasions, so the central government did not care to monitor them closely.
   d. The Persian king always put his biggest rivals at the periphery of his kingdom and gave them more autonomy to prevent rebellion.

5. What did the walled garden called "paradayadam" (paradise) symbolize to the Persians?
   a. The prosperity that the king and empire brought to loyal followers
   b. The divinity of the king
   c. The superiority of the leisure class
   d. The biblical garden of Eden

6. Which group of Persian workers received the most pay?
   a. Men
   b. Women
   c. Pregnant women
   d. Children

7. For the Greeks and other peoples living around it, the Mediterranean was
   a. a barrier.
   b. somewhat of a barrier.
   c. a connector.
   d. irrelevant.

8. Which of the following did *not* help inaugurate the outward-looking seafaring activities of the Greek Archaic period?
   a. Scarcity of resources
   b. The competition between Athens and Sparta
   c. The difficulty of overland trade
   d. The availability of good anchorages

9. When the Greeks developed their alphabet, it
   a. was probably used for economic purposes, such as keeping inventories.
   b. may have been originally used to write theatrical plays.
   c. brought about immediate literacy to Greek society.
   d. was so difficult to use that only scribes could learn it.

10. Which of the following about Greek colonies is *not* true?
    a. The colonists set out after receiving a blessing from the goddess Athena.
    b. Some colonists did not go willingly.
    c. Colonies provided a population safety valve.
    d. Colonists often reduced the native populations of their new colonies to a servile status.

11. What was the central ritual of Greek religion?
    a. Baptism
    b. Sacrifice
    c. Fasting
    d. Feasting

12. Why is Herodotus considered the "father of history"?
    a. He wrote many narratives of Greek events.
    b. He was the first person to record history.
    c. He was the first Greek to get paid to teach history.
    d. He sought the causes behind historical events.

13. To the Persians the conflict with the Greeks
    a. was all-consuming.
    b. was very important to the survival of their kingdom.
    c. was less important than it was to the Greeks.
    d. seemed inconsequential.

14. What enabled the rowers of Athenian battleships to gain an equal voice in the democratic system?
    a. The Hoplite Revolt
    b. The war with the Minoans
    c. A vote in the Athenian Assembly
    d. The great importance of the navy to the Athenian military

15. What motivated the theft of Alexander the Great's corpse by members of the Ptolemaic dynasty?
    a. They wanted to denigrate and humiliate the former Greek empire of Alexander.
    b. The theft was an attempt to gain legitimacy for Ptolemaic rule by claiming Alexander's blessing.
    c. They believed it would prove to their rivals that they had the military capability to carry out such a great scheme.
    d. They believed his corpse would bring them good fortune.

Short-Answer Questions

Answer each question in one short paragraph, giving the definition, dates, and significance.

1. What perception do modern historians have of the Persians, and why?

2. What was the ethnic makeup of the Iranians? Did it influence the history of Iran?

3. Compare and contrast Assyrian and Persian propaganda. Which was more effective? Why?

4. Why was the Greek alphabet an improvement over the writing systems of the Mesopotamians, the Egyptians, and even the Phoenicians?

5. How did Athens take advantage of its imperial status?

6. Discuss the career of Plato, suggesting reasons for some of the choices he made. What were his views? How can he be seen as a transitional figure?

7. Discuss women's role in Athens. What status did they have? How did their lives compare with those of Spartan women?

Essay Questions

Make an outline for each question, listing the major points you want to discuss. Then write your practice essay, following your outline carefully and making sure that you do not skip any of your major points. At this time you will want to add the relevant dates and details that will make your essay persuasive and accurate.

1. Compare and contrast Greek and Persian civilizations. What cultural traits, religious beliefs, and social organizations separated them? Which of these attributes did they share?

2. Discuss the effect of the physical environment on Persia and Greece. What aspects of the geography and climate influenced the development of their societies?

3. Discuss the development of Greek philosophy from the pre-Socratic thinkers to the Sophists. How were these various philosophies received by the Greek people?

4. Compare and contrast Sparta and Athens. What differences and similarities can be seen in their histories, government systems, goals, and societies? How did they interact?

5. Discuss the legacy of Greece and Persia. What effect did they have on their neighbors and on their descendants?

Comparison Charts

Using information gathered from the text, fill in the blank areas of each chart with the relevant data pertaining to the regions and categories listed. (Not all blank areas will necessarily be used.)

Chart 5.1
TWO APPROACHES TO RELIGION

	God(s)	Cosmology	Basic Tenets	Morality/Sin	Practices	Role of Humans	Outside Influences	Older Traditions	Government Use
Persia: Zoroastrianism									
Greece									

Chart 5.2
PHASES OF GREEK HISTORY

	Dates	Defining Event	Population	Government System	Dominant Region	Society	Trade/ Economics	Technology	Religion	Foreign Affairs	Migration
Minoans											
Mycenae											
Dark Ages											
Archaic Greece											
Classical Greece											
Hellenistic Age											

Society and Culture

After reading "Society and Culture: Greeks and Egyptians in Hellenistic Egypt" in your text, answer the following additional questions.

What does Philista's letter to King Ptolemy tell us about subject-ruler relations? What are her expectations based on this relationship? According to the comments in this section, are these expectations reasonable?

Internet Assignment

Keywords: "Acropolis"

"the Gate of All Nations" or "Takt-e-Jamshid"

Both the Acropolis of Athens and the city of Persepolis, where the Gate of All Nations is located, were ceremonial centers. Use the above keywords to find web sites about these topics. You might want to consult the *History WIRED* image library on the Bulliet, *The Earth and Its Peoples* web site (refer to the preface of this study guide for information on how to locate the Bulliet home page).

How did the two monuments differ in size and location? How did they differ in style and building materials? What can account for these differences?

Internet Exploration

Theories abound about Atlantis, and hardly a month goes by without another television special on the subject. How good are these theories? Use the keywords "Lost continent of Atlantis" to see some of the better, and some of the more imaginative theories. Evaluate the scientific and historical evidence that is used to back up those theories. Why were the ancient Greeks so fascinated with the possibility of a lost continent? Why are we?

Map Exercises

On Outline Map 5.1, shade in these areas:

Greek colonization   Lydia
Phoenician colonization   Anatolia
Peloponnese   Ionia

Then plot the following:

Carthage   Phoenicia
Corinth   Mediterranean Sea
Crete

On Outline Map 5.2, shade in the Persian homeland and outline the growth of the Persian Empire to its greatest extent. Then plot the following:

Susa   Royal Road
Persepolis   Lydia

Outline Map 5.1

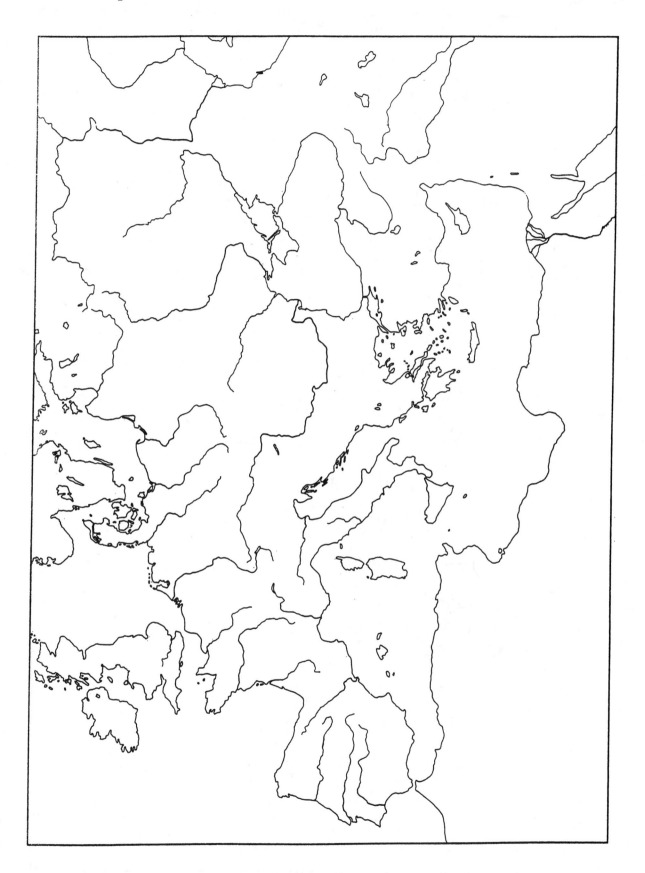

Outline Map 5.2

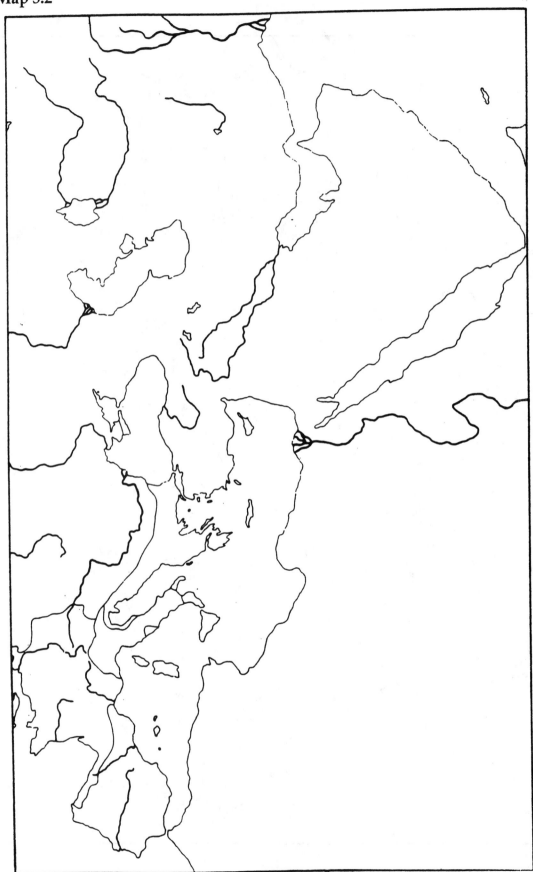

CHAPTER 6

An Age of Empires: Rome and Han China, 753 B.C.E.–330 C.E.

Learning Objectives

After reading Chapter 6 and completing this study chapter, you should be able to explain:

- How two great empires at opposite ends of the Eurasian continent could develop similar social attributes in answer to similar environmental and political challenges.

- How the Silk Road promoted trade of goods and ideas between the two empires through intermediaries but never linked their peoples directly.

- How Christianity in Rome and Confucianism in China helped define their respective cultures and shape the destinies of these empires.

- What factors may have contributed to the fall of Rome and Han China, and what factors may have allowed China to continue as a cohesive cultural system, while Rome eventually evolved into a collection of discrete states.

Chapter Outline

In the outline below, include important themes, concepts, and details in the blank spaces provided. If you find fewer points than you have space for, leave lines blank. If you find more points, add as many lines as necessary.

   I. **Introduction**

       A. *Two new empires: Rome and Han China*

          1. _____

          2. _____

          3. _____

B.   *Largest empires the world had seen to that point* _____

    1.   _____

    2.   _____

    3.   _____

C.   *Isolation* _____

    1.   _____

    2.   _____

    3.   _____

II.   **Rome's Creation of a Mediterranean Empire, 753** B.C.E.**–330** C.E.

A.   *A Republic of Farmers* _____

    1.   *City of Rome* _____

        a.   _____

        b.   _____

        c.   _____

    2.   *Agriculture* _____

        a.   _____

        b.   _____

        c.   _____

    3.   *Roman Republic and social structure* _____

        a.   _____

        b.   _____

        c.   _____

        d.   _____

        e.   _____

f. _____

g. _____

4. _Roman women_ _____

   a. _____

   b. _____

   c. _____

5. _Religion_ _____

   a. _____

   b. _____

   c. _____

B. _Expansion in Italy and the Mediterranean_ _____

   1. _What forces may have propelled expansion?_ ___

      a. _____

      b. _____

      c. _____

      d. _____

      e. _____

   2. _Roman conquest of Italy_ _____

      a. _____

      b. _____

      c. _____

   3. _Keys to success_ _____

      a. _____

      b. _____

c.   _____

4.   *Expansion outside of the Mediterranean* _____

    a.   _____

    b.   _____

    c.   _____

C.   *The Failure of the Republic* _____

1.   *Causes of failure* _____

    a.   _____

    b.   _____

    c.   _____

2.   *A series of ambitious individuals* _____

    a.   _____

    b.   _____

    c.   _____

3.   *Octavian (Augustus)* _____

    a.   _____

    b.   _____

    c.   _____

4.   *Countryside and land ownership* _____

    a.   _____

    b.   _____

    c.   _____

5.   *Commerce, trade, and Romanization* _____

a. _____

b. _____

c. _____

d. _____

e. _____

f. _____

D. *An Urban Empire* _____

   1. *Upper classes* _____

      a. _____

      b. _____

      c. _____

   2. *Poor Romans* _____

      a. _____

      b. _____

      c. _____

   3. *Municipal aristocracy* _____

      a. _____

      b. _____

      c. _____

E. *The Rise of Christianity* _____

   1. *Jesus and the Apostles* _____

      a. _____

      b. _____

      c. _____

2.   *Paul used cosmopolitan nature of the empire to spread Christianity* _____

    a. _____

    b. _____

    c. _____

3.   *Growth of Christianity* _____

    a. _____

    b. _____

    c. _____

F.   *Technology and Transformation* _____

   1.   *Technological advancements and military reorganization* _____

    a. _____

    b. _____

    c. _____

    d. _____

    e. _____

    f. _____

   2.   *"Third-century crisis" 235–284 C.E.* _____

    a. _____

    b. _____

    c. _____

    d. _____

    e. _____

    f. _____

g. _____

h. _____

3. *Diocletian* _____

   a. _____

   b. _____

   c. _____

4. *Constantine* _____

   a. _____

   b. _____

   c. _____

   d. _____

   e. _____

   f. _____

IV. **The Origins of Imperial China, 221** B.C.E.–**220** C.E.

   A. *Resources and Population* _____

      1. *Agricultural production* _____

         a. _____

         b. _____

         c. _____

         d. _____

      2. *Taking advantage of an expanding population* _____

         a. _____

         b. _____

         c. _____

3. *Expansion* _____

   a. _____

   b. _____

   c. _____

   d. _____

B. *Hierarchy, Obedience, and Belief* _____

   1. *The basic unit of Chinese society was the family* _____

      a. _____

      b. _____

      c. _____

      d. _____

   2. *Confucianism was the basis of the value system* _____

      a. _____

      b. _____

      c. _____

      d. _____

      e. _____

   3. *Experiences of women are difficult to pinpoint* _____

      a. _____

      b. _____

      c. _____

   4. *Religion* _____

      a. _____

      b. _____

c. _____

C. *The First Chinese Empire* _____

   1. *The rise of Shi huangdi* _____

       a. _____

       b. _____

       c. _____

   2. *A successful totalitarian regime* _____

       a. _____

       b. _____

       c. _____

       d. _____

   3. *Qin building and standardization* _____

       a. _____

       b. _____

       c. _____

D. *The Long Reign of the Han* _____

   1. *Reconstructing the empire* _____

       a. _____

       b. _____

       c. _____

   2. *Chang'an* _____

       a. _____

       b. _____

c. _____

3. *"Son of Heaven" and the "Mandate of Heaven"* _____

    a. _____

    b. _____

    c. _____

    d. _____

    e. _____

4. *Government organization and the role of the gentry* _____

    a. _____

    b. _____

    c. _____

    d. _____

    e. _____

5. *Daoism* _____

    a. _____

    b. _____

    c. _____

E. *Technology and Trade* _____

1. *Metallurgy and weapons* _____

    a. _____

    b. _____

    c. _____

2. *Roads and waterways* _____

    a. _____

    b. _____

    c. _____

3. *Trade and commerce* _____

    a. _____

    b. _____

    c. _____

F. *Decline of the Han Empire* _____

  1. *Relations between settled Chinese and nomads* _____

      a. _____

      b. _____

      c. _____

      d. _____

      e. _____

      f. _____

  2. *Xiongnu* _____

      a. _____

      b. _____

      c. _____

  3. *Factors weakening the Han* _____

      a. _____

      b. _____

      c. _____

V. Imperial Parallels

A. *Similarities between Rome and Han China (subject heading does not appear in text)* _____

1. *Family and architecture* _____

   a. _____

   b. _____

   c. _____

2. *Expansion and administration* _____

   a. _____

   b. _____

   c. _____

3. *Technologies, towns, and defense* _____

   a. _____

   b. _____

   c. _____

   d. _____

   e. _____

B. *Differences (subject heading does not appear in text)* _____

   1. *Chinese attitude towards role of individual in the state* _____

      a. _____

      b. _____

      c. _____

      d. _____

      e. _____

      f. _____

   2. *Roman family* _____

a. _____

b. _____

c. _____

d. _____

e. _____

3. *Political and religious ideology in Rome and Han China* _____

a. _____

b. _____

c. _____

C. *New belief systems (subject heading does not appear in text)* _____

1. *Christianity and Buddhism* _____

a. _____

b. _____

c. _____

d. _____

VI. Conclusion

A. *The Qin Empire emerged rapidly—elements of unification already there* _____

1. _____

2. _____

3. _____

B. *Early Roman state had no precedents for empire* _____

1. _____

2. _____

3. _____

   C.   *Social order and then decline* _____

       1. _____

       2. _____

       3. _____

Identifications

Define each term and explain why it is significant, including any important dates.

	Identification	*Significance*
Roman Republic		
Roman Senate		
patron/client relationship		
Roman Principate		
Augustus		
equites		
pax romana		
Romanization		
Jesus		
Paul		
roads		

	Identification	*Significance*
aqueduct		
concrete		
third-century crisis		
Diocletian		
Constantine		
Constantinople		
Qin		
Shi Huangdi		
census		
Han		
Chang'an		
gentry		
Xiongnu		
Kong Fu Zi/Confucius		

Multiple-Choice Questions

Read the entire question, including *all* the possible answers. Then choose the *one* answer that best fits the question.

1. In agricultural societies, the basis of wealth is
   a. the peasants.
   b. the land.
   c. food.
   d. precious metals.

2. During the Roman Republic, all adult male citizens had the right to vote,
   a. and so there was equal representation.
   b. and so everyone was equally powerless.
   c. but the votes were weighted so that the votes of the wealthy counted for more.
   d. but the votes of poor men were not counted.

3. The term for Roman senators was
   a. one year.
   b. four years.
   c. twenty-five years.
   d. life.

4. In a legal sense, Roman women
   a. never ceased being children.
   b. were nearly equal to men.
   c. were completely equal to men.
   d. were equal only to poor men.

5. Which of the following provides the most convincing explanation for Rome's expansion?
   a. The Romans were greedy and aggressive.
   b. The Romans were only defending themselves.
   c. The Romans feared a surprise attack.
   d. The Romans loved the thrill of battle.

6. Why did people during the time of the Roman Republic become dependent on expensive, imported grain?
   a. The grain was of higher quality than domestic grain.
   b. Roman religion forbade agriculture.
   c. Large landowners preferred to graze cattle or grow cash crops.
   d. This dependence was necessary in order to import silk from China.

7. The missionary career of the Apostle Paul
   a. was mostly unsuccessful.
   b. exemplifies the cosmopolitan nature of the Roman empire.
   c. ended in imprisonment in India.
   d. was narrow because he limited his message to Jews only.

8. Aqueducts worked with the aid of
   a. human muscle power.
   b. donkeys.
   c. gravity.
   d. solar-powered pumps.

9. Why did the people of the Late Roman Empire revert to a barter economy?
   a. The kingdoms they were trading with did not use money.
   b. None of Rome's trading partners would accept Roman currency because they did not trust the Roman banking system.
   c. The emperors were cutting back on the precious metals in the coins, thereby causing them to be devalued.
   d. It was more efficient for an illiterate people.

10. Which of the following is *not* one of the reasons that Constantine moved the capital of the Roman Empire to Constantinople?
    a. The eastern Empire was more threatened by the possibility of invasion.
    b. The middle class of the eastern Empire was wealthier.
    c. There were few Christians in the eastern Empire, so there was more opportunity to gain new converts.
    d. The economic health of the eastern Empire, especially its urban centers, was much better.

11. Why did the majority of the Chinese population during the Han dynasty live in eastern China?
    a. They wanted access to sea trade and its accompanying wealth.
    b. The best farmland was concentrated in eastern China.
    c. They were more isolated from invasion from nomadic peoples there.
    d. The best Buddhist centers were in eastern China.

12. The Qin government abolished slavery because
    a. it thought that making people work for the state for free was immoral.
    b. slavery was against the tenets of both Confucianism and Buddhism.
    c. slaves did not pay taxes but free people did.
    d. it was forced to do so by the great slave revolt of 208 B.C.E.

13. Roads were originally built in Rome and China to
    a. facilitate trade.
    b. move troops.
    c. enable the construction of massive monuments.
    d. encourage migration.

14. When the Han took over, they
    a. completely reinstated the Zhou system.
    b. completely eradicated all remnants of Qin rule.
    c. retained the Qin system with minor modifications.
    d. retained the entire Qin system without change.

15. During the Han dynasty, the emperor's chief widow did what upon his death?
    a. Killed herself
    b. Took over direct rule of China
    c. Became a nun
    d. Got to choose a new emperor from among the male members of the ruling clan

16. China's most valuable commodity was
    a. silk.
    b. tea.
    c. porcelain.
    d. opium.

17. Which of the following does *not* represent one way in which the Chinese tried to control nomadic raids?
    a. They paid protection money.
    b. They placed friendly people around the border as a buffer.
    c. They tried to reason with the nomads, citing the Buddhist principle of nonviolence.
    d. They tried to beat the nomads in outright warfare.

Short-Answer Questions

Answer each question in one short paragraph, giving the definition, dates, and significance.

1. How did family relations create pervasive social cohesion in both Rome and Han China?

2. Compare and contrast the cities of Rome and Chang'an.

3. How did wealthy Roman citizens maintain power during the Republic? How does this compare with the methods of the Chinese gentry?

4. Compare and contrast the role and status of women in Han China and Rome. How did women's situation there compare with that in China during earlier times and with the situation of Mediterranean women?

5. Compare and contrast the daily lives, and particularly the dwellings, of the wealthy and the poor of Rome.

6. Discuss the career of Paul and the development of the early Christian church.

7. Describe the duties of the husband and father and the wife and mother in China.

8. Describe the philosophy of Legalism. On what concept was it based? How and when was it applied in China? How successful was it?

9. Discuss the role that nomadic peoples played in the history of both Rome and China. How did the settled peoples view the nomadic peoples? In what ways were they dependent on each other?

Essay Questions

Make an outline for each question, listing the major points you want to discuss. Then write your practice essay, following your outline carefully and making sure that you do not skip any of your major points. At this time you will want to add the relevant dates and details that will make your essay persuasive and accurate.

1. Compare and contrast the empires of Rome and Han China. How were they structured? What methods did they use to keep order and gain prosperity? How successful were they? What weaknesses eventually led to their downfall?

2. Discuss the importance of trade to Rome and China. Who were their trading partners, and what was traded? How vital was trade to the economy of each empire? How did each empire view trade?

3. Compare and contrast the three major philosophies of early China: Confucianism, Legalism, and Daoism. What views did they offer on the relationship between the people and the state? How did they claim to be able to control the populace? How did each propose to solve the problems of the time? What was their success rate?

4. Trace the rise of the Chinese empire from the Qin state through the end of the Han dynasty. What factors were influential in its rise and fall? Account for the continuity of the Chinese culture in the face of war and dynastic change. Why did this continuity not exist to such a great extent in Rome?

5. Compare and contrast the role of the individual in Rome and Han China. How did the individual function in the family? How did the view of the individual affect society?

Comparison Charts

Using information gathered from the text, fill in the blank areas of each chart with the relevant data pertaining to the regions and categories listed. (Not all blank areas will necessarily be used.)

Chart 6.1
ROME

	Roman Republic	Roman Empire
Dates		
Political Systems		
Sources of Elite Power		
Notable Rulers		
Slavery		
Social Structure		
Family Structure		
Religion		
Trade and Economics		
Laws		
Technology		
Citizenship		
Housing		
Women		
External Relations		
Expansion		
Internal Relations		
Demise		
Successful States		

Chart 6.2
HAN CHINA

	Qin Empire	Earlier Han	Later Han
Dates			
Political Systems			
Sources of Government Power			
Notable Rulers			
Slavery			
Social Structure			
Family Structure			
Religion/Philosophy			
Trade and Economics			
Laws			
Technology			
Women			
Internal Relations			
External Relations			
Expansion			
Successful States			

Society and Culture

After reading "Society and Culture: Slavery in Rome and China" in your text, answer the following additional questions.

How were slaves procured in Rome and China? What kinds of tasks were they generally subject to? Were slaves as essential in China as in Rome? Considering the above factors, analyze the relative position in each society that slaves had.

Internet Assignment

Keywords: "Roman Coliseum"

                        "the Great Wall of China"

Monumental architecture is an important component of civilization, and can serve many purposes. Use the above keywords to find web sites about the Roman Coliseum and the Great Wall. You might want to consult the *History WIRED* image library on the Bulliet, *The Earth and Its Peoples* web site (refer to the preface of this study guide for information on how to locate the Bulliet home page).

What purpose did the Roman Coliseum and the Great Wall serve in Rome and China? What kind of human power would it take to build such structures, and how might that power have been compelled and organized? How can these two structures be symbols of both identity and cruelty?

Internet Exploration

Ever wondered what it felt like to stand in the center of the Coliseum, facing a daunting enemy, with the roar of the crowd surrounding you? Use the keyword "gladiator" to look at some web sites on this Roman figure. You will also find many sites on modern American gladiators. What makes a society interested in these kinds of very dangerous games? Why were the Romans fascinated with fighting to the death? Why are Americans today fascinated with feats of strength and skills necessary to be good fighters?

Map Exercises

On Outline Map 6.1, shade in the Roman Empire at its greatest extent and also the Parthian Empire. Then plot Rome.

On Outline Map 6.2, shade in the area ruled by the Han dynasty and outline that ruled by the Qin dynasty. Then plot the following:

Chang'an   Monsoon winds
Silk Road
Great Wall

Outline Map 6.1

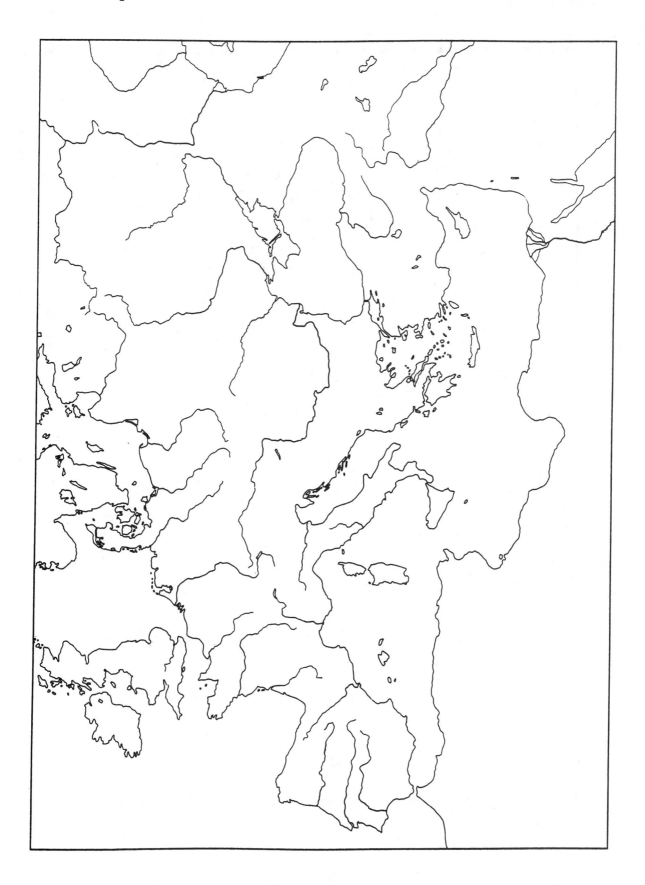

Outline Map 6.2

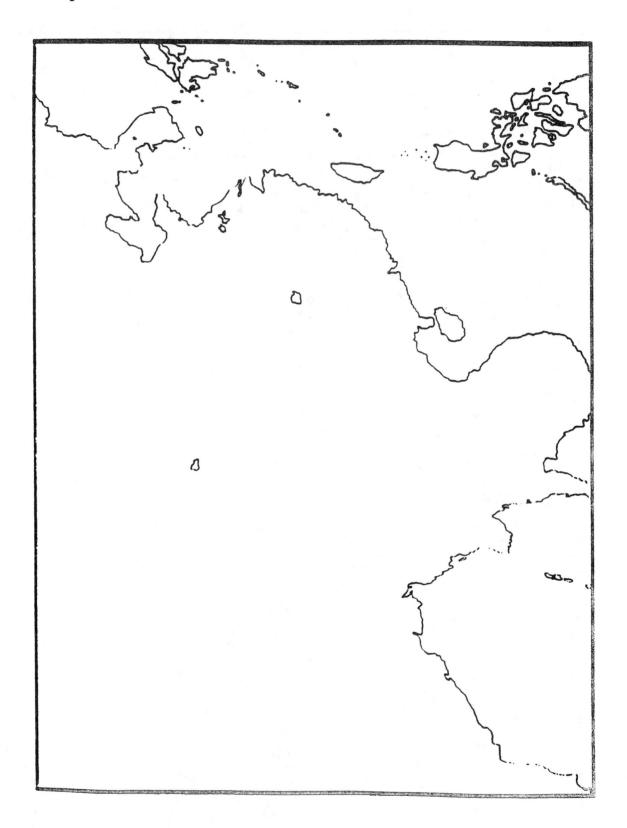

CHAPTER 7

India and Southeast Asia, 1500 B.C.E.–1100 C.E.

Learning Objectives

After reading Chapter 7 and completing this study chapter, you should be able to explain:

- In what ways the environments of India and Southeast Asia influenced the choice of the livelihood of the people, as well as the development of distinct social and governmental structures.

- How India evolved a complex social system and three distinct religious systems to meet the needs of its society.

- How the region of Southeast Asia developed into a major trading center, and how sophisticated government systems and social structures arose both from native traditions and as a result of outside influence from India and China.

- What Indian scientific and technological advancements developed between 1500 B.C.E. and 1100 C.E., and which of them still influence us today.

Chapter Outline

In the outline below, include important themes, concepts, and details in the blank spaces provided. If you find fewer points than you have space for, leave lines blank. If you find more points, add as many lines as necessary.

I. Introduction

    A. *Bhagavad-Gita—Krishna and Arjuna* _____

        1. _____

        2. _____

        3. _____

B. *Indian diversity* _____

   1. _____

   2. _____

   3. _____

C. *Role of religion in India* _____

   1. _____

   2. _____

   3. _____

II. **Foundations of Indian Civilization**

A. *The Indian Subcontinent* _____

   1. *Varied geography* _____

      a. _____

      b. _____

      c. _____

   2. *Monsoon* _____

      a. _____

      b. _____

      c. _____

   3. *Invasions and migration* _____

      a. _____

      b. _____

      c. _____

B. *The Vedic Age, 1500–500 B.C.E.* _____

1. *Indo-European migrations and fall of the Indus civilization*

   a. _____

   b. _____

   c. _____

2. *New technologies that aided migration*

   a. _____

   b. _____

   c. _____

3. *Conquest and blending of societies*

   a. _____

   b. _____

   c. _____

4. *Varna and jati*

   a. _____

   b. _____

   c. _____

   d. _____

   e. _____

5. *Religious beliefs and practices*

   a. _____

   b. _____

   c. _____

   d. _____

   e. _____

f. _____

6. *Women in ancient India* _____

    a. _____

    b. _____

    c. _____

C. *Challenges to the Old Order: Jainism and Buddhism* _____

  1. *Some people chose to retreat to forests* _____

    a. _____

    b. _____

    c. _____

  2. *Jainism* _____

    a. _____

    b. _____

    c. _____

  3. *Buddhism* _____

    a. _____

    b. _____

    c. _____

    d. _____

    e. _____

    f. _____

D. *The Rise of Hinduism* _____

  1. *Blending of traditions creates Hinduism* _____

    a. _____

    b. _____

    c. _____

    d. _____

2. *Gods and worshipers* _____

    a. _____

    b. _____

    c. _____

    d. _____

    e. _____

    f. _____

3. *Hinduism offers a variety of ways to approach God and worship* _____

    a. _____

    b. _____

    c. _____

III. Imperial Expansion and Collapse

A. *The Mauryan Empire, 324–184* B.C.E. _____

  1. *Chandragupta Maurya* _____

    a. _____

    b. _____

    c. _____

  2. *Administration* _____

    a. _____

    b. _____

      c. _____

   3.   *Ashoka* _____

      a. _____

      b. _____

      c. _____

B. *Commerce and Culture in an Era of Political Fragmentation* _____

   1.   *Domination by foreign powers and signs of development* _____

      a. _____

      b. _____

      c. _____

   2.   *Two Indian epics—the Ramayana and the Mahabharata* _____

      a. _____

      b. _____

      c. _____

      d. _____

   3.   *Bhagavad-Gita* _____

      a. _____

      b. _____

      c. _____

   4.   *Tamil kingdoms* _____

      a. _____

      b. _____

      c. _____

C. *The Gupta Empire, 320–550 C.E.* _____

1. *Consciously modeled on Mauryan Empire*

    a. _____

    b. _____

    c. _____

    d. _____

2. *Gupta control never as effective as Mauryan Empire*

    a. _____

    b. _____

    c. _____

3. *Decline in status of women*

    a. _____

    b. _____

    c. _____

    d. _____

    e. _____

4. *Trade*

    a. _____

    b. _____

    c. _____

IV. **Southeast Asia**

A. *Early Civilization*

    1. *Swidden agriculture*

        a. _____

        b. _____

        c. _____

  2. *Malay people's migrations* _____

        a. _____

        b. _____

        c. _____

        d. _____

        e. _____

  3. *The emergence of larger states* _____

        a. _____

        b. _____

        c. _____

        d. _____

        e. _____

  4. *Funan—first major Southeast Asian center* _____

        a. _____

        b. _____

        c. _____

        d. _____

B. *The Srivijayan Kingdom* _____

  1. *How Srivijaya gained ascendancy over its rivals* _____

        a. _____

        b. _____

        c. _____

        d. _____

   2. *The kings of Srivijaya* _____

        a. _____

        b. _____

        c. _____

        d. _____

        e. _____

   3. *The cultural influence of India was paramount* _____

        a. _____

        b. _____

        c. _____

V. Conclusion

  A. *Prominent place of religion in Indian society and concepts of time* _____

    1. _____

    2. _____

    3. _____

  B. *The tension between divisive and unifying forces* _____

    1. _____

    2. _____

    3. _____

  C. *Distinctive social and intellectual features* _____

    1. _____

    2. _____

    3. _____

Identifications

Define each term and explain why it is significant, including any important dates.

	Identification	*Significance*
monsoon		
Vedas		
varna		
jati		
karma		
moksha		
Buddha		
Mahayana Buddhism		
Theravada Buddhism		
atman		
reincarnation		
Hinduism		
Mauryan Empire		
Ashoka		
Mahabharata		
Bhagavad-gita		

	Identification	*Significance*
nirvana		
bhakti		
Vishnu		
Tamil kingdoms		
Malay peoples		
puja		
Gupta Empire		
theater-state		
water resource "boards"		
Funan		
Srivijaya		
Borobodur		
"Arabic" numerals		

Multiple-Choice Questions

Read the entire question, including *all* the possible answers. Then choose the *one* answer that best fits the question.

1. Indo-European nomads tended to be
   a. matriarchal.
   b. patriarchal.
   c. pacifist.
   d. agricultural.

2. Why did members of the higher castes fear contact with the lower castes?
   a. They feared pollution from contact with lower-caste individuals.
   b. The lower castes were believed to be a bad influence on upper-caste children.
   c. They did not want the lower castes to become Hindus.
   d. They wanted to retain Arya and Dasa blood purity.

3. Which of the following is *not* among the practices of Jainism?
   a. Strict nonviolence, emphasizing the holiness of the life force
   b. Farming in order to stay close to the land
   c. Extreme asceticism and nudity
   d. Eating so little so as to starve to death

4. After six years of strict asceticism, Siddhartha Gautama decided to
   a. commit suicide.
   b. enter nirvana.
   c. go home and resume his duties as a prince.
   d. adhere to a "Middle Path" of moderation.

5. Which of the following is *not* a characteristic of Buddhism?
   a. It denied the usefulness of gods.
   b. It demanded frequent sacrifices of small animals.
   c. It emphasized the search for spiritual truth.
   d. It focused on living one's life in a manner that minimized desire and suffering.

6. Why was the Buddha originally represented by symbols?
   a. Because it was more mystical
   b. So that his enemies would not recognize his temples and deface them
   c. To emphasize his achievement of a state of nonexistence
   d. Because Buddhism forbade the representation of all human forms

7. The incorporation of the Buddha into the Hindu pantheon
   a. was a blatant attempt to co-opt the rival religion's founder.
   b. indicated the open and all-encompassing nature of Hinduism.
   c. put an end to the rivalry between the followers of the two faiths.
   d. reflected the government's decision to patronize each religion equally.

8. Sacrifice is the major form of worship in
   a. Brahmanism.
   b. Buddhism.
   c. Hinduism.
   d. Jainism.

9. Which of the following factors did *not* contribute to a tendency toward disunity in ancient India?
   a. The different forms of organization and economic activity
   b. The threat of outside invasion
   c. The complex social hierarchy
   d. The landscape of India

10. What purpose did Ashoka's famous stone pillars serve?
    a. They were the first line of defense in India's wars with Persia.
    b. They were inscribed with his belief in nonviolence, morality, moderation, and religious tolerance both in government and in private life.
    c. They were actually burial markers.
    d. They were used to mark the rise and fall of the annual flooding of the Ganges River.

11. Why were several foreign kings in India more likely to convert to Buddhism than to Hinduism?
     a. Because Buddhism was a more optimistic religion
     b. Because the philosophy of Buddhism is easier to understand
     c. Because Hindu beliefs did not include reincarnation
     d. Because Hinduism had no easy mechanism for working foreigners into its system of class and caste

12. Which of the following is *not* part of Southeast Asia's three geographic zones?
     a. The Malay Peninsula
     b. The Japanese islands
     c. Thousands of islands extending on an east-west axis far out into the Pacific Ocean
     d. The Indochina mainland

13. The region of Southeast Asia first rose to prominence and prosperity because
     a. the two large kingdoms around it fell into ruin and decay.
     b. Europeans traded there.
     c. of its intermediary role in the trade between southern and eastern Asia.
     d. the land was unfit for agriculture and trade was the only way to make a living.

14. Which of the following crops did not originate in Southeast Asia?
     a. Taro
     b. Chickens
     c. Bananas
     d. Sugar cane

15. The most likely explanation for the decline of Funan in the sixth century is
     a. invasion by Chinese explorers.
     b. failure of its wet-rice crop.
     c. the marriage of its princess to an Indian Brahmin.
     e. International trade routes changed, bypassing Funan.

Short-Answer Questions

Answer each question in one short paragraph, giving the definition, dates, and significance.

1. Why do scholars focus on religious documents to understand ancient India?

2. What was the underlying message of the process of reincarnation?

3. Discuss the advances in science and technology in ancient India. What areas are of particular interest to India scholars? What major advancements were made?

4. Explain the Indian social pyramid. How did it come about? How is it manifested in Indian history? What is its purpose? How successful a social system is it?

5. What environmental benefits does Southeast Asia have? How did native peoples exploit those beneficial attributes?

6. Compare and contrast the Gupta Empire and the Srivijayan states. How did each control the population, raise money, and stay in power?

7. Why might Indians have come up with the concept of zero?

Essay Questions

Make an outline for each question, listing the major points you want to discuss. Then write your practice essay, following your outline carefully and making sure that you do not skip any of your major points. At this time you will want to add the relevant dates and details that will make your essay persuasive and accurate.

1. Trace the development of India from the Vedic era to the Mauryan dynasty and then to the Gupta Empire. Pay special attention to politics, religion, and social development. How did the status of women evolve in this time?

2. Compare and contrast Jainism and Buddhism. What were their basic beliefs and practices? What were they a response to? How successful were they?

3. Discuss the origins, evolution, and basic tenets of Hinduism. How did it affect people's daily lives? What political role has it played?

4. Discuss Southeast Asian migrations. Why did people migrate? Where did they go? How did they get there? What was the impact of their migrations?

5. Discuss Indian diversity. What groups make up Indian society? Is this diversity a drawback or an advantage? Explain. How does it relate to the great proliferation of gods, sects, and local practices in Hinduism?

6. What two outside factors influenced the development of large states in Southeast Asia? Name those states and trace their development.

Comparison Charts

Using information gathered from the text, fill in the blank areas of each chart with the relevant data pertaining to the regions and categories listed. (Not all blank areas will necessarily be used.)

Chart 7.1
WOMEN'S CHANGING ROLE IN INDIA

	Dates	Property/ Inheritance	Marriage/ Divorce	Religion	Education	Profession	Children	Freedom of Movement
Vedic Age								
Mauryan Empire								
Gupta Empire								

Chart 7.2
GROWTH OF SOUTHEAST ASIA

	Environment	Region	Dates	Social System	Trade/ Economics	Products	Technology	Religion	Outside Influence	Language	Monumental Architecture
Funan											
Srivijaya											

Society and Culture

After reading "Society and Culture: Reflections of the Status of Women in Indian Literature" in your text, answer the following additional questions.

In what ways does the king try to win Shakuntala's affections? What method finally works? What could this tell us about Shakuntala's self image and Indian women of Vedic times? Can we be sure?

Internet Assignment

Keywords: **"Hindu temples"**

                             "Borobudur"

In many societies the religious structures are the most prominent, and even long-lasting of all of the monuments created in the past. There are many fine examples of Indian Hindu temples, and many of them have a very similar shape to the temple at Borobudur. Use the above keywords to find web sites about the Indian Hindu temples and Borobudur. You might want to consult the *History WIRED* image library on the Bulliet, *The Earth and Its Peoples* web site (refer to the preface of this study guide for information on how to locate the Bulliet home page).

What do they tend to resemble? Did you find a reason for their shape? Compare and contrast the Indian Hindu temples and Borobudur. What might account for any similarities and differences?

Internet Exploration

One of the most interesting areas of study in any society is the various gods and goddesses. Indian deities are usually thought of as anthropomorphic (humanlike). Use the keywords "Hindu gods goddesses" to see many examples of Hindu deities. In what ways are they like humans? In what ways are they clearly not? What could account for some of the extraordinary forms that the gods and goddesses take?

Map Exercises

On Outline Map 7.1, shade in the Mauryan Empire and the Gupta Empire at their greatest extent and also the Kushan Empire. Then plot the following:

Pataliputra   Ganges River

On Outline Map 7.2, shade in the Srivijayan Empire, Champa, and Annam. Then plot Srivijaya, and Borobodur.

Outline Map 7.1

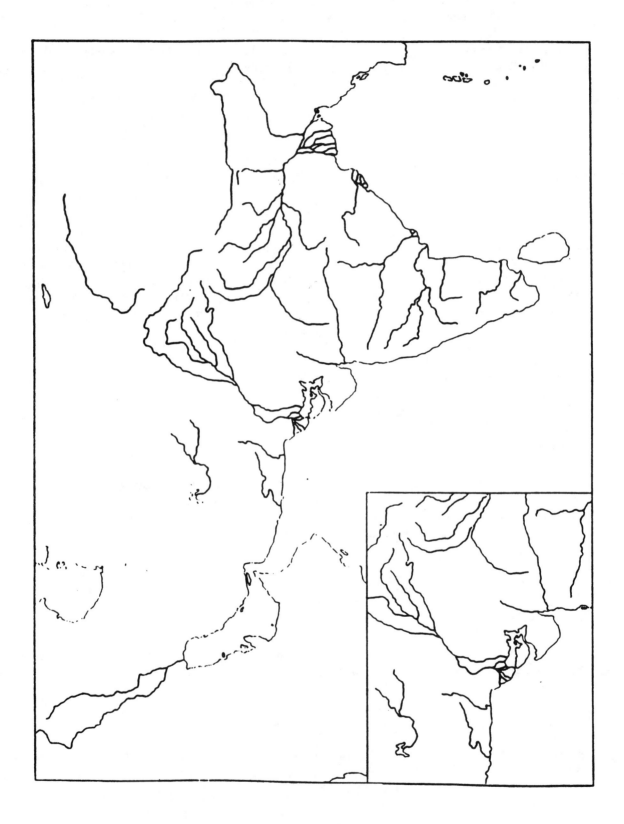

Outline Map 7.2

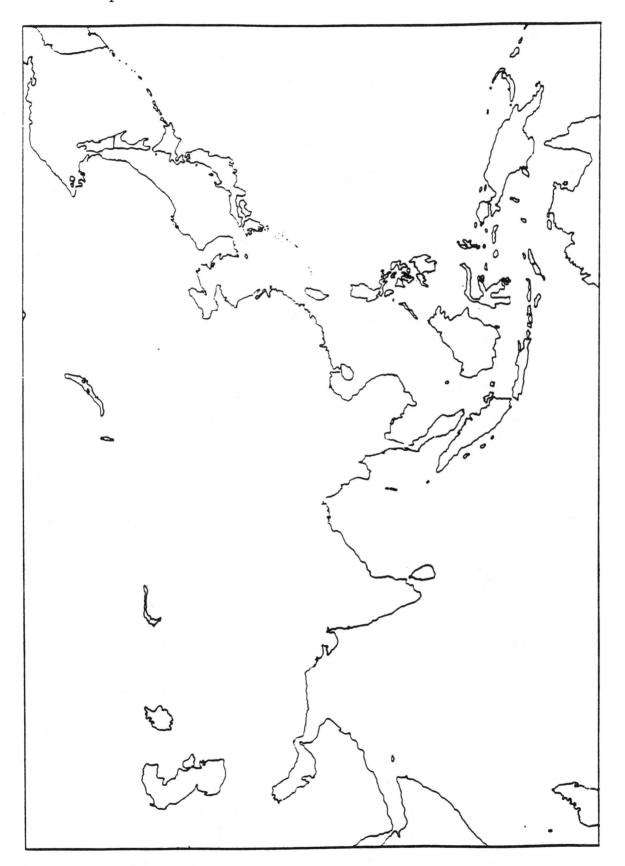

CHAPTER 8

Networks of Communication and Exchange, 300 B.C.E.–1100 C.E.

Learning Objectives

After reading Chapter 8 and completing this study chapter, you should be able to explain:

- How the Silk Road functioned as a conduit for goods, technology, and ideas, providing a link between far-flung empires and diverse peoples.

- How the Indian Ocean system transformed the regions of Africa, the Middle East, China, and Southeast Asia into a major trade network operated by Chinese and Muslim sailors.

- How even though the Sahara was a barrier to trade, it still permitted the transfer of vital goods and technology.

- How the migrations of the Bantu provided Africa with an underlying cultural unity, and what legacy this has left Africans.

- What impact the growth and spread of Buddhism and Christianity had on the peoples of Eurasia and Africa.

Chapter Outline

In the outline below, include important themes, concepts, and details in the blank spaces provided. If you find fewer points than you have space for, leave lines blank. If you find more points, add as many lines as necessary.

    I. Introduction

        A. *The Silk Road fostered exchange of goods, ideas, and people*

            1. _____

            2. _____

3. _____

B. *Links between wealthy elites and trade* _____

   1. _____

   2. _____

   3. _____

C. *The traders* _____

   1. _____

   2. _____

   3. _____

II. The Silk Road

A. *Origins and Operations* _____

   1. *The Partians encouraged trade along the Silk Road* _____

      a. _____

      b. _____

      c. _____

   2. *Chinese origins and General Zhang* _____

      a. _____

      b. _____

      c. _____

   3. *Occasional travel, migration, or trade?* _____

      a. _____

      b. _____

      c. _____

4. *Camels* _____

   a. _____

   b. _____

   c. _____

   d. _____

   e. _____

   f. _____

5. *Silk Road products* _____

   a. _____

   b. _____

   c. _____

B. *The Impact of Silk Road Trade* _____

   1. *Prosperity* _____

      a. _____

      b. _____

      c. _____

   2. *Military advances* _____

      a. _____

      b. _____

      c. _____

   3. *Social changes* _____

      a. _____

      b. _____

      c. _____

III. The Indian Ocean

A. *The Indian Ocean Maritime System*

1. *The "discovery" of the monsoon winds*

a. _____

b. _____

c. _____

2. *Sailing traditions of Indian Ocean peoples*

a. _____

b. _____

c. _____

3. *Indian Ocean colonies*

a. _____

b. _____

c. _____

B. *Origins of Contact and Trade*

1. *Migrations from Southeast Asia to Madagascar*

a. _____

b. _____

c. _____

2. *Agriculture and food crops*

a. _____

b. _____

c. _____

3. *Historians find it difficult to write the history of the Indian Ocean maritime system*

    a. _____

    b. _____

    c. _____

C. *The Impact of Indian Ocean Trade*

1. *Products and regions of their origin*

    a. _____

    b. _____

    c. _____

    d. _____

    e. _____

    f. _____

2. *Different areas have greater and lesser focus on seafaring and port cities*

    a. _____

    b. _____

    c. _____

    d. _____

    e. _____

    f. _____

3. *Social impact of traders despite lack of political power*

    a. _____

    b. _____

    c. _____

IV. Routes Across the Sahara

A. *Early Saharan Cultures*

1. *Evidence for the existence of early Saharan culture and lack of method to date evidence*

a. _____

b. _____

c. _____

d. _____

e. _____

2. *Hunters and new societies based on cattle breeding blend*

a. _____

b. _____

c. _____

d. _____

e. _____

3. *Horse herders arrive next—chariots?*

a. _____

b. _____

c. _____

d. _____

e. _____

B. *The Coming of the Camel*

1. *Saharan trade may be related to camel domestication*

a. _____

b. _____

c. _____

2. *Mention of camels in Latin sources (46 B.C.E.) and region of origin of camels*

    a. _____

    b. _____

    c. _____

3. *Evidence of south-to-north diffusion of camels and effect of spread*

    a. _____

    b. _____

    c. _____

    d. _____

    e. _____

B. *Trade Across the Sahara*

1. *The slow development of trade—south*

    a. _____

    b. _____

    c. _____

2. *The development of trade in the north*

    a. _____

    b. _____

    c. _____

3. *Changing patterns in north and Berber revolts*

    a. _____

    b. _____

c. _____

d. _____

e. _____

4. *Salt for gold* _____

   a. _____

   b. _____

   c. _____

   d. _____

C. *The Kingdom of Ghana* _____

1. *Ghana inaugurates the portion of political history of West Africa that can be documented* _____

   a. _____

   b. _____

   c. _____

2. *Ghanan kings* _____

   a. _____

   b. _____

   c. _____

3. *Takeover by Almoravids* _____

   a. _____

   b. _____

   c. _____

   d. _____

   e. _____

V. Sub-Saharan Africa

A. *A Challenging Geography*

1. *Cultural unity despite many geographic obstacles to movement*

a. _____

b. _____

c. _____

d. _____

B. *The Development of Cultural Unity*

1. *Cultural unity of Sub-Saharan Africa rested on "small traditions"*

a. _____

b. _____

c. _____

d. _____

2. *Diversity more apparent than unity*

a. _____

b. _____

c. _____

d. _____

e. _____

f. _____

3. *No outsiders could impose unity*

a. _____

b. _____

c. _____

B.   *African Cultural Characteristics*

   1.   *Kingship*

      a.   _____

      b.   _____

      c.   _____

   2.   *"Africanity"*

      a.   _____

      b.   _____

      c.   _____

   3.   *Climatic changes related to cultural unity*

      a.   _____

      b.   _____

      c.   _____

C.   *The Advent of Iron and the Bantu Migrations*

   1.   *Early iron smelting in Africa*

      a.   _____

      b.   _____

      c.   _____

   2.   *Bantu migrations and linguistic analysis*

      a.   _____

      b.   _____

      c.   _____

   3.   *Connection between Bantu migrations and iron smelting*

a. _____

b. _____

c. _____

VI. The Spread of Ideas

A. *Ideas and Things* _____

   1. *Pig domestication, consumption, and taboo* _____

     a. _____

     b. _____

     c. _____

   2. *Connection between domestication of pigs and religion* _____

     a. _____

     b. _____

     c. _____

   3. *Coins as a medium of exchange* _____

     a. _____

     b. _____

     c. _____

B. *The Spread of Buddhism* _____

   1. *King Ashoka* _____

     a. _____

     b. _____

     c. _____

   2. *Faxian* _____

     a. _____

    b. _____

    c. _____

    d. _____

    e. _____

    f. _____

3. *Missionaries to Syria, Egypt, Macedonia, and Southeast Asia* _____

    a. _____

    b. _____

    c. _____

4. *Theravada and Mahayana* _____

    a. _____

    b. _____

    c. _____

    d. _____

B. *The Spread of Christianity* _____

  1. *The spread of Christianity to Armenia* _____

    a. _____

    b. _____

    c. _____

  2. *The spread of Christianity in Ethiopia* _____

    a. _____

    b. _____

    c. _____

3.   *The patriarch of Alexandria* _____

    a.   _____

    b.   _____

    c.   _____

VII.   Conclusion

    A.   *Differences between impact of trade and folk migrations* _____

      1.   _____

      2.   _____

      3.   _____

    B.   *However, ideas did spread well via trade* _____

      1.   _____

      2.   _____

      3.   _____

Identifications

Define each term and explain why it is significant, including any important dates.

	Identification	*Significance*
Silk Road		
nomads		
Parthians		
stirrup		
silk		
caravan cities		

	Identification	*Significance*
camels		
Indian Ocean Maritime System		
Trans-Saharan caravan routes		
Sahel		
Ghana		
Sub-Saharan Africa		
rock painting		
steppes		
Savanna		
Tropical rain forest		
great traditions		
small traditions		
Bantu		
salt		
Armenia		
Ethiopia		

Multiple-Choice Questions

Read the entire question, including *all* the possible answers. Then choose the *one* answer that best fits the question.

1. Which of the following statements about those who traveled along the Silk Road is *not* true?
   a. They were well respected by the local townspeople.
   b. They were nomads.
   c. They were secretive about their knowledge.
   d. They contributed more to the drawing together of the world than most kings.

2. Emperor Wu of Han dynasty China sent out an expedition headed by General Zhang Jian in 128 B.C.E. to
   a. defeat the Xiongnu.
   b. make diplomatic overtures to the Scythians.
   c. explore trade possibilities with caravan cities.
   d. acquire paper-making technology from the Turks.

3. Which of the following was *not* one of the technologies that originated in Central Asia?
   a. Chariot warfare
   b. The camel saddle
   c. The use of mounted bowmen
   d. Use of stirrups

4. What did the Chinese want to import?
   a. A variety of Western goods, especially horses
   b. Porcelain
   c. Greek incense
   d. Nothing to import—only to trade for cash

5. The monsoon winds that facilitate sailing across the Indian Ocean were discovered by
   a. the Greek Hippalus.
   b. the Phoenicians.
   c. the Chinese.
   d. the peoples living in Africa, the Arabian peninsula, India, and the Malay Peninsula.

6. Which of the following factors do *not* explain Africa's persisting diversity?
   a. Sub-Saharan Africa covered a huge area with tremendous diversity of climate, terrain, and vegetation.
   b. Low population density allowed substantial spatial separation between groups, discouraging rigid cultural uniformity.
   c. Massive military incursions by the Egyptians divided Africa into distinct political and cultural regions.
   d. No external conqueror was able to penetrate the region's natural barriers to impose a thin veneer of culture on tribal peoples.

7. Why did the individual ruling families of the independent Central Asian caravan cities not try to overthrow their neighbors and form an empire?
   a. It would have been bad for business.
   b. They were not strong enough militarily.
   c. The Chinese would never have allowed it.
   d. Buddhism did not permit such action.

8. Which of the following is *not* one of the ways in which scholars trace cultural similarities and migration patterns of sub-Saharan African peoples?
   a. Anthropology
   b. Oral history
   c. Accounts of the "small traditions"
   d. Written history

9. Evidence for the south-to-north adoption of camel use comes from
   a. written sources.
   b. studies of camel saddle design.
   c. studies of camel breeding techniques.
   d. folktales.

10. What sub-Saharan desert product was in particularly great demand in the torrid regions?
    a. Ivory
    b. Salt
    c. Kola nuts
    d. Gold

11. Ghana means
    a. the "land of gold."
    b. the "refuge of Islam."
    c. the "land of plenty."
    d. the "crossroads of trade."

12. The island of Madagascar was settled by
    a. Africans only.
    b. Africans and Asians.
    c. Asians only.
    d. Polynesians.

13. How did the Berbers use camels in warfare?
    a. They shot arrows while mounted.
    b. They only used them for trade, not warfare.
    c. They dismounted and used them as shields.
    d. They ate them.

14. What evidence did pilgrims encounter that attested to the long history of Buddhist preaching and conversion along the Silk Road?
    a. The proliferation of Buddhist communities and temples in caravan cities
    b. The writings of Marco Polo
    c. The pillars erected by Ashoka
    d. The spread of Buddhism left no physical evidence

15. Which of the following can probably be attributed to the desiccation of the Sahara?
    a. The Bantu migrations
    b. The emergence of the Old Kingdom of Egypt
    c. The fall of Rome
    d. The migration to Madagascar

Short-Answer Questions

Answer each question in one short paragraph, giving the definition, dates, and significance.

1. What kinds of peoples carried on the trade in caravans and on the sea?

2. Discuss the role of women in the Indian Ocean maritime societies.

3. Define and discuss the terms *great traditions* and *small traditions*. Why are such terms potentially biased?

4. Describe African kingship. What are its attributes? How does this system affect Africa?

5. Why is sub-Saharan Africa's cultural unity less apparent than its cultural diversity?

6. Using Africa as your example, explain how linguistics is used to trace the development and distribution of peoples.

7. Describe the process involved in the domestication of the camel and its impact for trade. Were camels used for anything else?

Essay Questions

Make an outline for each question, listing the major points you want to discuss. Then write your practice essay, following your outline carefully and making sure that you do not skip any of your major points. At this time you will want to add the relevant dates and details that will make your essay persuasive and accurate.

1. Compare and contrast the lifestyles and livelihoods of settled and nomadic peoples. What technologies did each employ? What geographic features did each have to address?

2. Discuss the institution of the Silk Road. How did it work? Who ran it? What were some of the things that traveled along the Silk Road? How did it influence those who came into contact with it?

3. Compare and contrast the Mediterranean maritime world and the Indian Ocean maritime system prior to the arrival of European explorers in the fifteenth century C.E.

4. Describe the development and the mechanics of the trans-Saharan trading system. How did it differ from the maritime systems of the Mediterranean and Indian Ocean?

5. Trace the spread of Buddhism from the second to the eighth century C.E. Did the advent of the so-called "great traditions" such as Buddhism and Christianity completely displace local customs, traditions, and social formations? What was the role of the "great traditions"?

Comparison Charts

Using information gathered from the text, fill in the blank areas of each chart with the relevant data pertaining to the regions and categories listed. (Not all blank areas will necessarily be used.)

Chart 8.1
CROSS-CULTURAL CONTACTS

	Geographic Regions	Livelihood	Housing	Technology	Possessions	Source of Wealth	Population	Government Structure	Contact with Opposite Group
Settled Peoples									
Nomads									

Chart 8.2
TRADE ROUTES

	Who Traded	Where	Transportation	Goods	Technology	Ideas	Impact
Silk Road							
Indian Ocean Trading Basin							
Sub-Saharan African Routes							

Society and Culture

After reading "Society and Culture: Caravan Cities" in your text, answer the following additional questions.

What kind of lifestyle do the inhabitants of caravan cities enjoy and why? Why do you think there is so much "democracy" in Petra?

Internet Assignment

Keywords: **"Ashoka"**

                        "Mansa Musa Mali"

Many leaders actively promoted the spread of religion during their reigns. Use the above keywords to find web sites about Ashoka and Mansa Musa Mali. You might want to consult the *History WIRED* image library on the Bulliet, *The Earth and Its Peoples* web site (refer to the preface of this study guide for information on how to locate the Bulliet home page).

Both Ashoka and Mansa Musa helped to gain converts to Buddhism and Islam respectively. What methods did they use? How did their styles differ? What were any long-term effects of their efforts?

Internet Exploration

The Silk Road was a major thoroughfare for trade during the empires of Rome and Han China. But many scholars think that the Silk Road's origins may date back much earlier, in fact as much as two thousand years earlier. Use the keywords "Mummies Xinjiang Province" to see some evidence of early trade and travel along the legendary Silk Road. A specific site you may enjoy is www.pbs.org/wgbh/nova/chinamum/taklamakan.html. What kinds of people traveled the Silk Road, and why were scholars so surprised about their identity?

Map Exercises

On Outline Map 8.1, plot the following:

Silk Road   Malay Peninsula
Rome   India
Ferghana   Yellow River
Indian Ocean

Shade in these areas:

Roman Empire   Region of Mongols
Han dynasty China   Region of Turkic nomads
Kushan Empire

Show the spread of Buddhism by marking the original center in fifth century B.C.E. and shading in the areas to which Buddhism spread in these periods:

Fifth to third century B.C.E.

Second century B.C.E. to tenth century C.E.

Third to second century B.C.E.

On Outline Map 8.2, shade in the following:

Sub-Saharan Africa

The historical kingdom of Ghana

East Africa

Outline Map 8.1

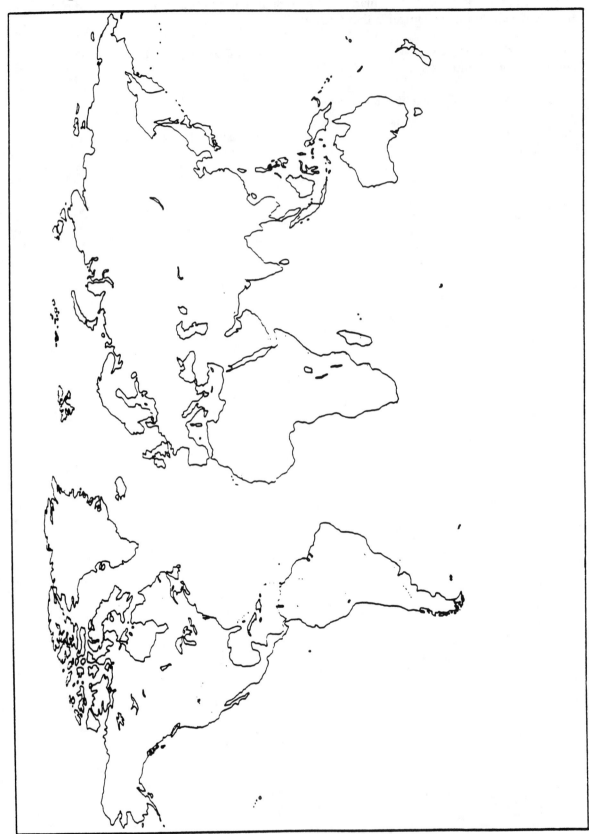

Outline Map 8.2

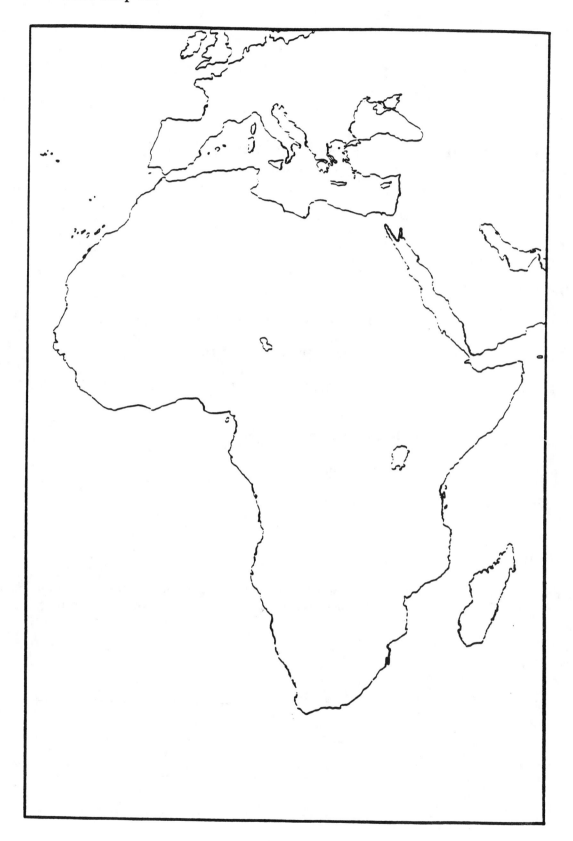

CHAPTER 9

The Sasanid Empire and the Rise of Islam, 200–1200

Learning Objectives

After reading Chapter 9 and completing this study chapter, you should be able to explain:

- How Islam originated, and how other traditions have influenced its development.

- How Islamic society developed secular rule, and how the institution of the caliphate evolved over time.

- What role the Quran and the hadith had in Muslim law and society.

- What influence Islam exerted on women, families, and slavery.

- How Islamic life differed in urban and rural areas.

Chapter Outline

In the outline below, include important themes, concepts, and details in the blank spaces provided. If you find fewer points than you have space for, leave lines blank. If you find more points, add as many lines as necessary.

I. Introduction

    A. *The meaning of Muhammad's blessing of Ali* _____

        1. _____

        2. _____

        3. _____

    B. *A division within the Muslim community* _____

    1. _____

    2. _____

    3. _____

C. *Islam and empire* _____

    1. _____

    2. _____

    3. _____

II. **The Sasanid Empire 224–651**

A. *Politics and Society* _____

    1. *Both Sasanids and Byzantines used Arabs to protect their empires from invasion*

        a. _____

        b. _____

        c. _____

    2. *Rivalry and trade between Sasanid and Byzantine Empires*

        a. _____

        b. _____

        c. _____

    3. *Arab role and prosperity* _____

        a. _____

        b. _____

        c. _____

    4. *Aristocratic rule and stability* _____

        a. _____

        b. _____

        c. _____

B.   *Religion and Empire* _____

    1.   *Zoroastrianism established as the state religion* _____

        a. _____

        b. _____

        c. _____

    2.   *Christians became pawns in the political rivalry with Byzantines* _____

        a. _____

        b. _____

        c. _____

    3.   *Manichaeism* _____

        a. _____

        b. _____

        c. _____

        d. _____

    4.   *The politicizing of religion* _____

        a. _____

        b. _____

        c. _____

III. The Origins of Islam

A.   *The Arabian Peninsula Before Muhammad* _____

    1.   *Life in the southern regions of the peninsula* _____

        a. _____

b. _____

c. _____

2.   *Caravan trading* _____

a. _____

b. _____

c. _____

3.   *Mecca* _____

a. _____

b. _____

c. _____

d. _____

e. _____

B.   *Muhammad in Mecca* _____

1.   *Muhammad's revelations* _____

a. _____

b. _____

c. _____

2.   *Arab religious beliefs: jinns and shaitans* _____

a. _____

b. _____

c. _____

3.   *The beliefs of Islam and its early success* _____

a. _____

b. _____

c. _____

d. _____

e. _____

f. _____

C. *The Formation of the Umma* _____

   1. *The flight (hijra) to Medina* _____

     a. _____

     b. _____

     c. _____

   2. *Creation and leadership of the umma* _____

     a. _____

     b. _____

     c. _____

   3. *The defeat of Mecca and the succession of leadership* _____

     a. _____

     b. _____

     c. _____

   4. *Abu Bakr* _____

     a. _____

     b. _____

     c. _____

   5. *Ali and the Shi'ites* _____

     a. _____

b. _____

c. _____

d. _____

e. _____

f. _____

IV. The Rise and Fall of the Caliphate, 632–1258

A. *The Islamic Conquests, 634–711* _____

   1. *Conquests up through the eighth century* _____

     a. _____

     b. _____

     c. _____

   2. *Why the conquests were so successful* _____

     a. _____

     b. _____

     c. _____

     d. _____

     e. _____

     f. _____

   3. *Umar's policies regarding land and army* _____

     a. _____

     b. _____

     c. _____

B. *The Umayyad and Early Abbasid Caliphates, 661–850* _____

   1. *Development and characteristics of the Umayyad Caliphate* _____

a. _____

b. _____

c. _____

2. *The decline of the Umayyad Caliphate* _____

  a. _____

  b. _____

  c. _____

3. *The development of the Abbasid Caliphate* _____

  a. _____

  b. _____

  c. _____

4. *Abbasid cultural developments* _____

  a. _____

  b. _____

  c. _____

  d. _____

  e. _____

  f. _____

C. *Political Fragmentation, 850–1050*

1. *Difficult to rule an empire stretching one quarter of the way around the world* _____

  a. _____

  b. _____

  c. _____

2.   *Internal problems encourage breakup of caliphate and the rise of new states*

    a. _____

    b. _____

    c. _____

    d. _____

    e. _____

    f. _____

3.   *States of Spain, Morocco, and Algeria*

    a. _____

    b. _____

    c. _____

    d. _____

    e. _____

    f. _____

D.   *Assault from Within and Without, 1050–1258*

   1.   *Nomadic migrations into Africa, Syria, and Iraq*

    a. _____

    b. _____

    c. _____

    d. _____

    e. _____

    f. _____

   2.   *Turkish rule*

    a. _____

b. _____

c. _____

d. _____

e. _____

f. _____

3. *The Crusades and Saladin* _____

   a. _____

   b. _____

   c. _____

4. *The Mongol conquests* _____

   a. _____

   b. _____

   c. _____

V. Islamic Civilization

A. *Law and Dogma* _____

1. *The development of law* _____

   a. _____

   b. _____

   c. _____

2. *The hadith* _____

   a. _____

   b. _____

   c. _____

3. *The Shari'a* _____

    a. _____

    b. _____

    c. _____

B. *Converts and Cities* _____

  1. *Conversion and education of new Muslims* _____

    a. _____

    b. _____

    c. _____

  2. *Cities were the centers of Islam* _____

    a. _____

    b. _____

    c. _____

    d. _____

    e. _____

    f. _____

  3. *Science and medicine flourished* _____

    a. _____

    b. _____

    c. _____

C. *Islam, Women, and Slaves* _____

  1. *Seclusion and veiling of women* _____

    a. _____

    b. _____

c. _____

2. *Legal rights of women* _____

   a. _____

   b. _____

   c. _____

3. *Slavery* _____

   a. _____

   b. _____

   c. _____

D. *The Recentering of Islam* _____

   1. *Influence of Iranian Muslims and the madrasa* _____

      a. _____

      b. _____

      c. _____

   2. *Sufi brotherhoods* _____

      a. _____

      b. _____

      c. _____

   3. *Twelfth- and thirteenth-century transition* _____

      a. _____

      b. _____

      c. _____

VI. Conclusion

A. *Islam culminated the transition from identity based on ethnicity to one based on religion* _____

1. _____

2. _____

3. _____

B. *Changes in growth and leadership* _____

1. _____

2. _____

3. _____

C. *New religious institutions* _____

1. _____

2. _____

3. _____

Identifications

Define each term and explain why it is significant, including any important dates.

	Identification	*Significance*
Shi'ites		
Sunnis		
Sasanid Empire		
Mecca		
Muhammad		
Ali		

	Identification	*Significance*
Abu Bakr		
muslim		
Islam		
Medina		
umma		
caliphate		
Quran		
A'isha		
Umayyad Caliphate		
Abbasid Caliphate		
mamluks		
ulama		
Shari'a		
hadith		
madrasa		

Multiple-Choice Questions

Read the entire question, including *all* the possible answers. Then choose the *one* answer that best fits the question.

1. What role was *not* played by Arab pastoralists in the relationship between the Sasanid and Byzantine Empires?
   a. They were recruited as elite military personnel.
   b. They became part of imperial politics and culture.
   c. They supplied camels and guides.
   d. They were merchants and organizers of caravans.

2. What did the proclamation of Christianity and Zoroastrianism as official faiths symbolize?
   a. It foreshadowed the dominance of monotheism.
   b. It marked the emergence of religion based on the struggle between the forces of light and darkness.
   c. It indicated the decline of the Sasanid and Byzantine Empires.
   d. It marked the emergence of religion as an instrument of politics.

3. In the Muslim view, Judaism and Christianity
   a. were heretical religions.
   b. were negligent in preserving God's word.
   c. were useful only politically.
   d. were equal in value to Islam.

4. Why did Muslims change the direction of their prayer from Jerusalem to Mecca?
   a. They did so to differentiate between themselves and the Jews of Medina.
   b. They made the change to show respect to the angel Jibra'il.
   c. It was a political move to strengthen them in the battle between Mecca and Medina.
   d. They did not change it; it had always been directed toward Mecca.

5. The supremacy of the Medinan state was based on
   a. kinship.
   b. common faith in a single god.
   c. military might.
   d. trade.

6. To which factor can we attribute the success of the spread of the Muslim empire?
   a. The leniency of Islam toward Jews and Christians.
   b. The warfare between the Sasanid and Byzantine Empires, which weakened these two empires.
   c. The fact that the caliphs who guided the conquests were both sophisticated and inspired by Muhammad.
   d. Muhammad's military genius.

7. Which of the following statements best describes the Arab Muslims' relationship to their subject peoples?
   a. They required all their subjects to convert, and they forced conversion by the sword if necessary.
   b. They required all their subjects to convert, but they offered ample financial rewards for conversion.
   c. There was an extensive missionary effort to encourage conversion.
   d. Arabs were a minority, and they did not have the ability to force their faith on those they conquered.

8. Which of the following factors did *not* contribute to the decline of the Umayyad dynasty?
   a. New converts to Islam felt that they deserved equal status with the privileged Arab warriors.
   b. The Umayyad ban on trade caused economic hardship.
   c. Pious Muslims felt that the Umayyad family behaved immorally.
   d. The Shi'ites and the Kharijites contested the Umayyad family's claim to rule on religious grounds.

9. As Islam developed, it
   a. remained untouched by outside influences.
   b. evolved but remained untouched by outside influences.
   c. was changed dramatically by local traditions.
   d. absorbed many "little traditions," which allowed it to be more adaptable.

10. The hadith
   a. is a book of the Quran.
   b. provided a valuable supplement to the Quran, adding material on legal issues not covered there.
   c. is a collection of sayings that challenge the authority of the Quran.
   d. provided legitimacy to the Shi'ite movement.

11. The practice of secluding and veiling women
   a. has its roots in the Christian society of the Byzantine Empire.
   b. has its roots in the Quran.
   c. has its roots in one of the "little traditions" of the Muslim world.
   d. is actually a twentieth-century development and is a reaction to Western intrusion.

12. A hereditary slave society never developed in the Islamic world because
   a. slaves usually converted to Islam, often causing their masters to free them, and the offspring of slave women and Muslim men were free.
   b. the only people Muslims enslaved were Jews, Christians, and Zoroastrians, and they were scarce in the Middle East.
   c. slavery of Muslims was illegal according to the Quran.
   d. all slavery was illegal according to the Quran.

Short-Answer Questions

Answer each question in one short paragraph, giving the definition, dates, and significance.

1. Describe the relationship between the Sasanid and Byzantine Empires.

2. Describe the occurrences on "The Night of Power and Excellence."

3. What are some of the reasons suggested by historians for the spread of Islam and the expansion of the Muslim empire?

4. How did mass conversion of conquered peoples change the way in which the umma perceived itself?

5. Discuss the position of women in Muslim societies, paying particular attention to the issues of seclusion, veiling, and education. How did the status of Muslim women compare with that of Jewish and Christian women?

Essay Questions

Make an outline for each question, listing the major points you want to discuss. Then write your practice essay, following your outline carefully and making sure that you do not skip any of your major points. At this time you will want to add the relevant dates and details that will make your essay persuasive and accurate.

1. Describe the religious atmosphere in Byzantium and the Arabian Peninsula before the rise of Islam. How did Islam change the outlook and behavior of the peoples from this region?

2. Describe the system of succession for the leadership of Islam. How did it originate and why? How did the schism occur, and what was its impact on Islam?

3. How did the Abbasid caliphate differ in style and substance from the Umayyad caliphate?

4. Discuss the decline of the institution of the caliphate. Why did it decline, and what were the results of that decline?

Comparison Charts

Using information gathered from the text, fill in the blank areas of each chart with the relevant data pertaining to the regions and categories listed. (Not all blank areas will necessarily be used.)

Chart 9.1
JUDAISM, CHRISTIANITY, AND ISLAM

	God(s)	Afterlife	Sin and Judgment	Practices	Leaders	Political Views	Texts	Society	Law
Judaism									
Christianity									
Islam									

Chart 9.2
UMAYYAD AND ABBASID

	Dates	Capital	Founder(s)	Outlook	Style	Challengers to Conquer	Role of Religion	Decline
Umayyad								
Abbasid								

Society and Culture

After reading "Society and Culture: The Fraternity of Beggars" in your text, answer the following additional questions.

What was the lifestyle of the beggars, and how is that reflected in the poem? How do the beggars feel about their profession, and people outside of the beggar community?

Internet Assignment

Keyword: "Richard I"

                  "Saladin"

During the Crusades, and sometimes even since then, Christians and Muslims have dehumanized each other during times of conflict. Truthfully, both sides contributed vast resources to the passionate cause of the Crusades, and both sides created heroes. Two heroes on opposite sides that managed to gain the respect even of the "enemy" were Richard I of England (or Richard the Lionheart) and Saladin, a Kurd fighting on the Muslim side. Use the above keywords to find web sites about these two men. You might want to consult the *History WIRED* image library on the Bulliet, *The Earth and Its Peoples* web site (refer to the preface of this study guide for information on how to locate the Bulliet home page).

How were the aims of these two men similar? How were they different? Does the way their portraits were drawn in the past influence our opinion of them today?

Internet Exploration

People living in the West view the veiling of Muslim women as repressive and demeaning. Muslims, including Muslim women, often do not share this view. Explore Muslim and non-Muslim opinions on veiling by using the keywords "women Islam veil" or "hijab." Why do many Muslim women voluntarily practice veiling? Does the practice of "hijab" (modest dress and behavior) apply only to women? How do people who practice veiling view the clothing styles of Western peoples?

Map Exercise

On Outline Map 9.1, shade the areas of Muslim expansion under Muhammad during these periods:

622–632
632–661
661–750

Outline the areas controlled by the following:

Umayyad Caliphate
Abbasid Caliphate
Muslims in Cordoba, Spain

Outline Map 9.1

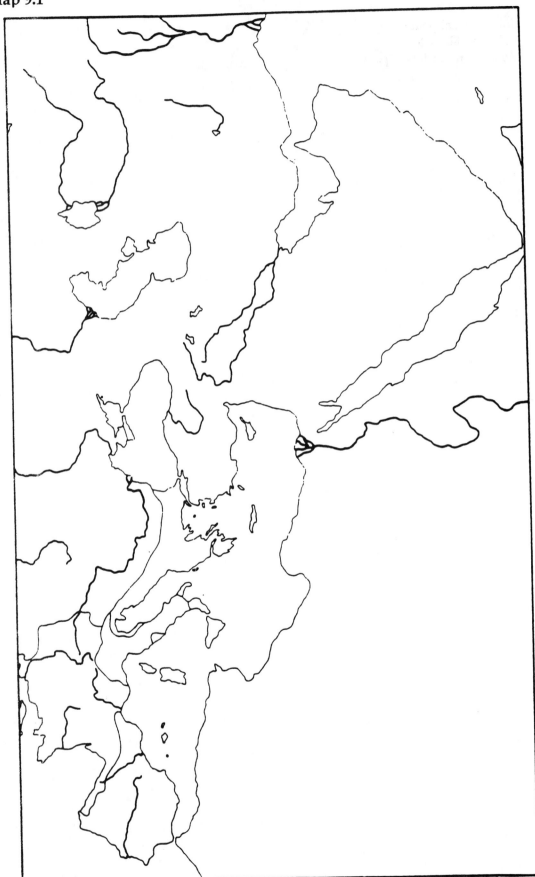

CHAPTER 10

Christian Europe Emerges, 300–1200

Learning Objectives

After reading Chapter 10 and completing this study chapter, you should be able to explain:

- How European society evolved from the remnants of the Roman Empire, eventually combining Roman tradition, Christianity, and Germanic culture into a distinctive society.

- What role the Latin Church played in western Europe, and how it compared with the role played by the Byzantine Church.

- How the paths of the former western Roman Empire and the Byzantine Empire diverged and why.

- What role technology and improvements in agriculture played in the development of the European economy.

- How Kievan Russia developed both in conjunction with Western Europe and Byzantium, yet developed distinctive characteristics.

Chapter Outline

In the outline below, include important themes, concepts, and details in the blank spaces provided. If you find fewer points than you have space for, leave lines blank. If you find more points, add as many lines as necessary.

I. Introduction

    A. *Charlemagne crowned Emperor of Rome*

        1. _____

        2. _____

3. _____

B. *Shift away from Mediterranean to northern and western Europe* _____

   1. _____

   2. _____

   3. _____

C. *Byzantine Empire's success* _____

   1. _____

   2. _____

   3. _____

II. **Early Medieval Europe 300–1000**

   A. *From Roman Empire to Germanic Kingdoms* _____

      1. *Rome's decline and shift eastward* _____

         a. _____

         b. _____

         c. _____

      2. *Western Rome breaks up politically and linguistically* _____

         a. _____

         b. _____

         c. _____

      3. *New invasions and Carolingians* _____

         a. _____

         b. _____

         c. _____

      4. *Vikings* _____

    a. _____

    b. _____

    c. _____

    d. _____

    e. _____

B. *A Self-Sufficient Economy* _____

  1. *A move toward self-sufficiency* _____

    a. _____

    b. _____

    c. _____

    d. _____

    e. _____

    f. _____

  2. *The manor as self-sufficient farming estates* _____

    a. _____

    b. _____

    c. _____

  3. *Manors and personal status* _____

    a. _____

    b. _____

    c. _____

C. *Early Medieval Society* _____

  1. *The evolution from warrior to knight* _____

a. _____

b. _____

c. _____

2.   *The technology of the mounted warrior* _____

a. _____

b. _____

c. _____

d. _____

e. _____

f. _____

3.   *Fiefs, vassals, and kings* _____

a. _____

b. _____

c. _____

4.   *Women* _____

a. _____

b. _____

c. _____

d. _____

III.   The Western Church

A.   *The Structure of the Christian Faith* _____

1.   *The patriarchates* _____

a. _____

b. _____

    c. _____

  2. *Different views on rituals and beliefs* _____

    a. _____

    b. _____

    c. _____

    d. _____

    e. _____

    f. _____

  3. *Schisms, Arianism and orthopraxy* _____

    a. _____

    b. _____

    c. _____

    d. _____

    e. _____

    f. _____

B. *Politics and the Church* _____

  1. *The alliance between the pope and secular leaders* _____

    a. _____

    b. _____

    c. _____

  2. *The investiture controversy* _____

    a. _____

    b. _____

c. _____

d. _____

3. *Henry II and increasing royal power* _____

a. _____

b. _____

c. _____

d. _____

e. _____

f. _____

4. *Western Europe heir to three different legal traditions* _____

a. _____

b. _____

c. _____

C. *Monasticism* _____

1. *Origins* _____

a. _____

b. _____

c. _____

2. *The Rule of Benedict* _____

a. _____

b. _____

c. _____

3. *The function of monasteries and nunneries* _____

a. _____

b. _____

c. _____

d. _____

e. _____

f. _____

4. *The Cluniac Movement* _____

   a. _____

   b. _____

   c. _____

   d. _____

C. *Shaping European Society* _____

1. *Christian influence on morals* _____

   a. _____

   b. _____

   c. _____

2. *Christian influence regarding Jews* _____

   a. _____

   b. _____

   c. _____

3. *Christian influence on the family and Germanic tastes* _____

   a. _____

   b. _____

   c. _____

IV. **The Byzantine Empire, 300–1200**

    A. *Church and State* _____

        1. *Continuity from the old Roman Empire in Byzantium* _____

            a. _____

            b. _____

            c. _____

        2. *Patriarchs and polytheism* _____

            a. _____

            b. _____

            c. _____

        3. *Threats to political unity and loss of power* _____

            a. _____

            b. _____

            c. _____

            d. _____

            e. _____

            f. _____

    B. *Society and Urban Life* _____

        1. *Seventh-century decline* _____

            a. _____

            b. _____

            c. _____

        2. *Decline in status of all but royal women* _____

            a. _____

b. _____

c. _____

3. *Constantinople* _____

    a. _____

    b. _____

    c. _____

C. *Cultural Achievements* _____

1. *Justinian's Legal Code* _____

    a. _____

    b. _____

    c. _____

2. *Architecture—the Hagia Sophia* _____

    a. _____

    b. _____

    c. _____

3. *The development of Cyrillic* _____

    a. _____

    b. _____

    c. _____

V. Kievan Russia, 900–1200

A. *The Rise of the Kievan State* _____

1. *Princes and trade* _____

    a. _____

    b. _____

c. _____

2. *The adoption of Orthodox Christianity as the official religion of the Kievan Russ* _____

   a. _____

   b. _____

   c. _____

3. *Vladimir's marriage and his own conversion* _____

   a. _____

   b. _____

   c. _____

   d. _____

   e. _____

   f. _____

B. *Society and Culture* _____

   1. *Agriculture* _____

      a. _____

      b. _____

      c. _____

   2. *Urban centers* _____

      a. _____

      b. _____

      c. _____

   3. *Christianity* _____

      a. _____

b. _____

c. _____

d. _____

e. _____

VI. **Western Europe Revives, 1000–1200**

   A. *The Role of Technology* _____

      1. *Brought about dramatic increase in population* _____

         a. _____

         b. _____

         c. _____

      2. *Technology boosted economy* _____

         a. _____

         b. _____

         c. _____

      3. *The use of horses replaced oxen in agriculture* _____

         a. _____

         b. _____

         c. _____

   B. *Cities and the Rebirth of Trade* _____

      1. *Independent cities* _____

         a. _____

         b. _____

         c. _____

         d. _____

e. _____

f. _____

2. *Venice* _____

   a. _____

   b. _____

   c. _____

3. *Cities in Flanders: Ghent, Bruges, and Ypres* _____

   a. _____

   b. _____

   c. _____

4. *Coinage* _____

   a. _____

   b. _____

   c. _____

C. *The Crusades* _____

1. *The culmination of social and economic currents of the eleventh century* ____

   a. _____

   b. _____

   c. _____

   d. _____

   e. _____

   f. _____

2. *Pilgrimage* _____

   a. _____

b. _____

c. _____

3. *"The Muslim threat"* _____

    a. _____

    b. _____

    c. _____

VII. Conclusion

A. *Western Rome fell* _____

    1. _____

    2. _____

    3. _____

B. *Other empires and rise of Islam* _____

    1. _____

    2. _____

    3. _____

C. *Byzantium and continued Roman traditions* _____

    1. _____

    2. _____

    3. _____

Identifications

Define each term and explain why it is significant, including any important dates.

	Identification	*Significance*
Charlemagne		
medieval		
Byzantine Empire		
manor		
serfs		
nobles		
fief		
vassal		
papacy		
schism		
Holy Roman Empire		
investiture controversy		
monasticism		
Rule of Benedict		
Kievan Russia		
horse collar		

| | *Identification* | *Significance* |

Hagia Sophia

Cyrillic

Crusades

pilgrimage

Druzhina

Multiple-Choice Questions

Read the entire question, including *all* the possible answers. Then choose the *one* answer that best fits the question.

1. The crowning of Charlemagne as emperor of the Romans by the pope symbolized
    a. the rise of a new Roman Empire.
    b. a shift in focus away from the Mediterranean and toward northern Germanic Europe.
    c. a shift away from secular rule and toward theocracy.
    d. the new power of the papacy.

2. Why is the period in Europe between 500 C.E. and 1300 C.E. called the "Middle Ages"?
    a. It came between the Greco-Roman civilization and the Renaissance.
    b. Europe at this time was controlled by peoples in its central area rather than by the people of the Mediterranean as it had been in the past.
    c. It was the beginning of the rise of the middle class.
    d. Europe was invaded by Muslim nomads from the Middle East.

3. Which of the following was *not* a unifying force in the chaotic remains of the western Roman Empire?
    a. Germanic family-based law
    b. The Roman judicial system
    c. Slavic religious tradition
    d. The Christian Church

4. Which of the following factors did *not* prompt the growth of the great fortified manors?
    a. Religious wars
    b. Isolation due to poor communication networks
    c. Political insecurity
    d. Warfare and instability, which made manors the target of raiders

5. How did improvements in armor dictate changes as to who could become a mounted knight?
   a. As armor became heavier, only those who were particularly physically fit could fight with it on.
   b. As armor became one of the items imported from China, only those in trading cities or the sons of merchants could obtain it.
   c. As armor became more expensive, only knights who had financial support from land revenues could afford to outfit themselves properly.
   d. As armor became more effective, fewer soldiers were required, and so only a select few were chosen to fight.

6. Which of the following statements about noblewomen in medieval Europe is *not* true?
   a. Noblewomen became enmeshed in the tangle of feudal obligations through marriage.
   b. Noblewomen lived powerless, sheltered lives.
   c. Noblewomen were guarded by noblemen as part of their prized possessions.
   d. Some noblewomen exercised real power, administering their husband's lands when they were away at war.

7. What was the investiture controversy?
   a. A disagreement about the standards for choosing the pope
   b. A conflict between popes and kings regarding control of ecclesiastical offices
   c. A disagreement about how knights should be chosen
   d. A conflict between the various kings regarding the legality of parliaments

8. Most ancient works in Latin would have disappeared if
   a. some classical person had not hidden hundreds of them away in caves.
   b. ninth-century monks had not copied them.
   c. Muslim invaders had not carried them off to their homelands as booty.
   d. they had not become popular as relics.

9. Which of the following statements best characterizes the influence of Roman traditions in Byzantium?
   a. Byzantium carried on the traditions of Rome almost without interruption.
   b. Byzantium made a dramatic break with Roman tradition, as did Western Europe.
   c. Byzantium was influenced so much by Islam that it gradually rejected Roman traditions.
   d. Byzantium carried on the traditions of Rome but mixed them freely with Germanic traditions.

10. Why is it paradoxical that women ruled the Byzantine Empire together with their husbands from 1028 to 1056?
    a. Roman family structure was traditionally loose, and women had been comparatively active in public life.
    b. Byzantine women increasingly found themselves confined to their homes and required to veil themselves in public.
    c. The law code gave women no political rights.
    d. The patriarch said that women should work only in the home.

11. Why did Kievan Russians decide to adopt Orthodox Christianity?
    a. They were impressed by the magnificence of Constantinople.
    b. They were betrayed by Jewish Khazars, and so rejected Judaism.
    c. The Slavs revolted, demanding they adopt Orthodox Christianity.
    d. Actually, they chose Islam instead.

12. Which of the following technological innovations probably did not play a significant role in the launching of the economy of Western Europe after the year 1000?
    a. an improved horse collar.
    b. the importation of a superior plow from the Mediterranean.
    c. the development of a plow that both cut and turned the soil.
    d. the use of teams of horses rather than oxen.

13. Which of the following is *not* one of the reasons usually offered by historians for the Crusades?
    a. The Church wanted to cut down on warfare between Christian lords and redirect it toward enemies of the Church.
    b. Ambitious lords were looking for new lands to conquer.
    c. Italian merchants wanted to increase trade.
    d. The Pope wanted to recapture the Holy Land.

Short-Answer Questions

Answer each question in one short paragraph, giving the definition, dates, and significance.

1. Discuss the role and impact of the Vikings in medieval Europe.

2. How did the institution of feudalism develop, and how did it operate?

3. Discuss marriage practices in medieval Europe. How did they vary by class, and how was marriage experienced differently by men and women?

4. Why were secular law and religious law on a collision course in medieval Europe?

5. What functions did monasteries and nunneries serve?

6. What were some of the changes that the Christian church underwent from Roman times to the Middle Ages?

7. Compare and contrast the role and position of women in Latin Europe and the Byzantine Empire.

8. Why did the institution of manorial agriculture never develop in Kievan Russia?

Essay Questions

Make an outline for each question, listing the major points you want to discuss. Then write your practice essay, following your outline carefully and making sure that you do not skip any of your major points. At this time you will want to add the relevant dates and details that will make your essay persuasive and accurate.

1. Describe the transition from Roman society to medieval society. Pay special attention to social, economic, religious, and political issues.

2. Discuss the conflicts between religious and secular authorities in medieval Europe. What form did the disagreements take, over what issues were they generated, and how were they resolved?

3. Compare and contrast the development of Latin Europe, Byzantium, and Kievan Russia, paying special attention to religion and political unity.

4. What improvements were made to help increase agricultural production in western Europe? How did these compare with agricultural techniques in Byzantium?

5. Discuss the growth of cities and the rebirth of trade. What led up to this development, and how was society affected?

6. The Crusades were a major event in Europe of the Middle Ages. Why were they conducted, who benefited from them, and how did they affect Christian-Muslim relations?

Comparison Charts

Using information gathered from the text, fill in the blank areas of each chart with the relevant data pertaining to the regions and categories listed. (Not all blank areas will necessarily be used.)

Chart 10.1
FROM ROMAN EMPIRE TO GERMANIC KINGDOMS

Regional Focus	Law	Political Structure	Church	Economy	Status and Role of Women	Decline
Rome						
Germanic Kingdoms						

Chart 10.2
LATIN WEST AND BYZANTINE EMPIRE

	Unity	Political Structure	Religious Structure	Social Structure	Trade and Economics	Status of Women	Decline
Latin West							
Byzantine Empire							

Society and Culture

After reading "Society and Culture: The Penitentials of Saint Patrick" in your text, answer the following additional questions.

What can be learned about early Christian views of "pagans" from this text? What was the Church's view, at that time, of the supernatural?

Internet Assignment

Keywords: "Viking ships"

                    "Hagia Sophia"

The contributions of the Vikings and the Byzantines, or Eastern Romans, have helped to form today's Western culture; they were however vastly different societies. Use the keywords above to find web sites about Viking ships and the Hagia Sophia. You might want to consult the *History WIRED* image library on the Bulliet, *The Earth and Its Peoples* web site (refer to the preface of this study guide for information on how to locate the Bulliet home page).

How are Viking ships the perfect symbol of Viking society? How is Byzantine society reflected in the Hagia Sophia? How have these structures been preserved until modern times?

Internet Exploration

Mystery and magic surround the written language of early Germanic peoples. Where are runes from? What do they mean? Are they magical? Go to http://www.pbs.org/wgbh/nova/vikings/runes2.html to learn more about runes and their uses. As a bonus, learn to write your name in runes!

Map Exercise

On Outline Map 10.1, trace the routes of the following:

Vikings   Second Crusade
Muslims   Third Crusade
Ostrogoths   Fourth Crusade
First Crusade

Shade in the boundaries of the following:

Islamic world, 600–800   Christian lands, 600–800
Crusader kingdoms in the East
Christian lands, 300–600

Outline Map 10.1

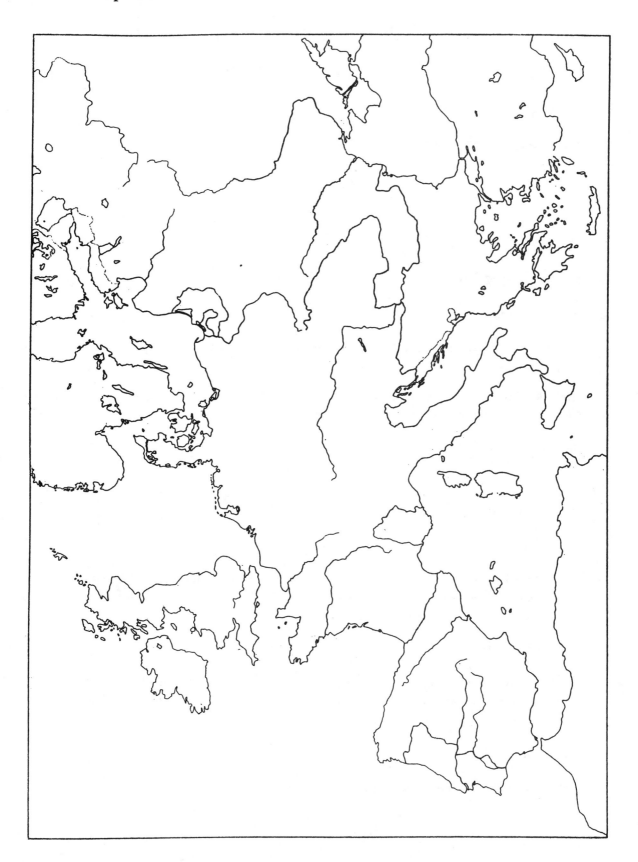

CHAPTER 11

Central and Eastern Asia, 400–1200

Learning Objectives

After reading Chapter 11 and completing this study chapter, you should be able to explain:

- How the Sui and Tang dynasties of China rose, fell, and influenced both later dynasties and the peoples around them.

- How Buddhism was received in the various East Asian and Central Asian countries, how it changed them, and in turn how they adapted and controlled it.

- In what ways the lifestyles of nomadic and sedentary peoples differed, and how geography influenced their choice of lifestyle.

- How the Song dynasty differed from earlier dynasties, and how it changed the outlook of the Chinese and influenced society.

- What the Song technological explosion comprised.

- What role Chinese culture played in the development of Korea, Japan, and Vietnam, and how each of them both adapted Chinese culture and retained their own distinct traditions.

Chapter Outline

In the outline below, include important themes, concepts, and details in the blank spaces provided. If you find fewer points than you have space for, leave lines blank. If you find more points, add as many lines as necessary.

I. Introduction

    A. *The fall of the Han dynasty and disunity* _____

        1. _____

2. _____

3. _____

B. *New inventions* _____

    1. _____

    2. _____

    3. _____

C. *Reunification* _____

    1. _____

    2. _____

    3. _____

II. **The Sui and Tang Empires, 581–755**

    A. *Reunification Under the Sui and Tang* _____

        1. *Sui achievements* _____

            a. _____

            b. _____

            c. _____

            d. _____

            e. _____

            f. _____

        2. *Sui downfall* _____

            a. _____

            b. _____

            c. _____

        3. *Rise of the Tang* _____

a. _____

b. _____

c. _____

d. _____

e. _____

f. _____

B. *Buddhism and the Tang Empire* _____

   1. *The political uses of Buddhism* _____

      a. _____

      b. _____

      c. _____

   2. *Mahayana Buddhism* _____

      a. _____

      b. _____

      c. _____

      d. _____

      e. _____

      f. _____

   3. *Spread of Buddhism* _____

      a. _____

      b. _____

      c. _____

C. *To Chang'an by Land and Sea* _____

1. *The city of Chang'an* _____

   a. _____

   b. _____

   c. _____

   d. _____

   e. _____

   f. _____

2. *Market networks of Chang'an* _____

   a. _____

   b. _____

   c. _____

   d. _____

   e. _____

   f. _____

3. *Trade by sea* _____

   a. _____

   b. _____

   c. _____

D. *Tang Integration* _____

1. *Outside influences from Iran and Central Asia* _____

   a. _____

   b. _____

   c. _____

   d. _____

e. _____

f. _____

2.   *Tang infrastructure* _____

a. _____

b. _____

c. _____

3.   *Tang products* _____

a. _____

b. _____

c. _____

E. *Fractured Power in Central Asia and China, to 907* _____

1.   *Relationship between China, Tibet, and the Uigurs* _____

a. _____

b. _____

c. _____

2.   *The effects on Tang China* _____

a. _____

b. _____

c. _____

3.   *Nomadic economies of Central Asia cushion the blow of social disorder and agricultural losses* _____

a. _____

b. _____

c. _____

F. *Reaction and Repression* _____

1. *Distrust of Buddhism by elites* _____

a. _____

b. _____

c. _____

d. _____

e. _____

f. _____

2. *Specific Buddhist policies and beliefs that upset the Chinese* _____

a. _____

b. _____

c. _____

d. _____

e. _____

f. _____

3. *Some Confucians feared Buddhism undermined Confucianism and the inferior role of women* _____

a. _____

b. _____

c. _____

d. _____

4. *Destruction of monasteries* _____

a. _____

b. _____

c. _____

G. *The End of the Tang Empire* _____

   1. *Disintegration of the political system and cultural decay* _____

      a. _____

      b. _____

      c. _____

   2. *The Huang Chao rebellion of 879–881 and the Chinese reaction* _____

      a. _____

      b. _____

      c. _____

      d. _____

      e. _____

      f. _____

   3. *The end of the Tang and its legacy* _____

      a. _____

      b. _____

      c. _____

H. *The Uigur and Tibetan Empires in Central Asia* _____

   1. *Turks* _____

      a. _____

      b. _____

      c. _____

   2. *Uigurs* _____

a. _____

b. _____

c. _____

d. _____

e. _____

f. _____

3. *Tibet* _____

   a. _____

   b. _____

   c. _____

   d. _____

   e. _____

   f. _____

III. The Emergence of East Asia, to 1200

A. *The Liao and Jin Challenge* _____

   1. *Northern empires allow multiple cultures* _____

      a. _____

      b. _____

      c. _____

   2. *The Khitan People (the Liao Empire)* _____

      a. _____

      b. _____

      c. _____

   3. *The Jurchens (the Jin Empire)* _____

a. _____

b. _____

c. _____

B. *Song Industries* _____

　　1. *Adapted from Tang information and technology* _____

a. _____

b. _____

c. _____

　　2. *Mathematics, astronomy, and timekeeping* _____

a. _____

b. _____

c. _____

d. _____

e. _____

f. _____

　　3. *Ships, seafaring, military, and metallurgy* _____

a. _____

b. _____

c. _____

C. *Economy and Society* _____

　　1. *Civil pursuits* _____

a. _____

b. _____

c. _____

2.   *The examination system* _____

    a. _____

    b. _____

    c. _____

    d. _____

    e. _____

    f. _____

3.   *Printing* _____

    a. _____

    b. _____

    c. _____

    d. _____

    e. _____

    f. _____

4.   *Cities* _____

    a. _____

    b. _____

    c. _____

    d. _____

    e. _____

5.   *Economic advances* _____

    a. _____

    b. _____

c. _____

d. _____

e. _____

f. _____

6. *Women* _____

    a. _____

    b. _____

    c. _____

    d. _____

    e. _____

    f. _____

E. *Essential Partners: Korea, Japan, and Vietnam* _____

1. *Korea* _____

    a. _____

    b. _____

    c. _____

    d. _____

    e. _____

    f. _____

    g. _____

2. *Japan* _____

    a. _____

    b. _____

    c. _____

d. _____

e. _____

f. _____

g. _____

   3. *Vietnam* _____

     a. _____

     b. _____

     c. _____

     d. _____

     e. _____

     f. _____

     g. _____

IV. Conclusion

A. *Tang unity* _____

   1. _____

   2. _____

   3. _____

B. *The emergence of regional cultures* _____

   1. _____

   2. _____

   3. _____

C. *Song achievements* _____

   1. _____

   2. _____

3. _____

4. _____

5. _____

6. _____

Identifications

Define each term and explain why it is significant, including any important dates.

	Identification	*Significance*
Chang'an		
Grand Canal		
Tang Empire		
Li Shimin		
tributary system		
Mahayana Buddhism		
bubonic plague		
Uigurs		
Song Empire		
junk		
gunpowder		
shamanism		

	Identification	*Significance*
Koryo		
Shinto		
examination system		
footbinding		
Trung sisters		
movable type		
Kamakura Shogunate		
Champa rice		

Multiple-Choice Questions

Read the entire question, including *all* the possible answers. Then choose the *one* answer that best fits the question.

1. The Sui Empire lasted such a short time because
    a. its rulers angered the gods.
    b. it was exhausted by its extraordinary pace of expansion and overcentralization.
    c. the last emperor, Yangdi, was an evil man.
    d. a series of violent storms flooded the capital city, Xian.

2. The purpose of the Grand Canal was to
    a. facilitate trade and communication within China.
    b. enhance China's ability to protect itself from foreign invasion.
    c. bring students into the capital to take the Imperial Examinations.
    d. irrigate rice paddies in northern China.

3. The main belief of Mahayana Buddhism was that
    a. life was suffering.
    b. bodhisattvas have postponed nirvana to help others achieve enlightenment.
    c. all should worship in their own language and according to their customs.
    d. monks should travel around converting many people to Buddhism.

4. How did the bubonic plague reach East Asia?
   a. It was brought by European Crusaders to the Middle East and then transmitted along the Silk Road to China.
   b. It traveled along the Grand Canal.
   c. It came from Africa, spread to West Asia, and then went by sea to Canton.
   d. It started in Japan, crossed the China Sea, then traveled by sea to Africa, and was carried by Moors into Spain.

5. Which of the following is *not* one of the ways that Buddhist institutions allied themselves with the Tang imperial family?
   a. Monastic leaders openly supported women as emperors.
   b. Monastic leaders prayed for aspiring Princes.
   c. Monks counseled aristocrats to support claimants to the throne.
   d. Monasteries contributed money to imperial war chests.

6. The Uigurs were famous as merchants and
   a. warriors
   b. diplomats
   c. mathematicians
   d. scribes

7. The most dramatic change in the status of Chinese women during the Song dynasty was manifested by
   a. the introduction of slavery.
   b. footbinding.
   c. veiling.
   d. the introduction of education for women.

8. Why did the Song Empire look east and south for allies?
   a. Korea, Japan, and Vietnam had been settled originally by Chinese people and so were very similar to China.
   b. Like Song China, the regions to the east and south formed one Confucian region.
   c. Areas north and west of China were hostile and seemed alien.
   d. It needed the people of these regions for military support.

9. Why was rice growing well suited to Confucian ideology?
   a. It demanded the cooperation of large kin groups.
   b. Rice was white, symbolizing ideological purity.
   c. Rice was easy to weigh and transport and so made taxation more efficient.
   d. Growing rice was so time consuming that peasants had no time to study for the Imperial Examinations.

10. Where was movable type originally developed?
    a. Europe
    b. China
    c. Japan
    d. Korea

11. Central Japan was most likely unified in the fourth or fifth century c.e. by
    a. indigenous Japanese tribes.
    b. Chinese invaders.
    c. Mongols.
    d. Korean warriors on horseback.

12. Japan during the eighth century can best be described as
    a. backward and underdeveloped.
    b. a "little China."
    c. warlike.
    d. a major Buddhist center, perhaps surpassing China.

13. The concept of the Mandate of Heaven was not important in Japan because
    a. Japan was less warlike than China.
    b. Confucianism was less accepted in Japan.
    c. Japanese rulers always came from the same family.
    d. the concept was never transmitted to Japan by Korea.

14. The early Annamese were probably *not* ahead of the Chinese in their
    a. mastery of certain forms of ceramics.
    b. use of draft animals in agriculture.
    c. military tactics.
    d. metalworking.

15. The combination of loneliness, free time, and writing encouraged Japanese women to
    a. produce an outpouring of poetry, diaries, and novels.
    b. form alliances with each other.
    c. become wandering nuns.
    d. commit suicide.

Short-Answer Questions

Answer each question in one short paragraph, giving the definition, dates, and significance.

1. Explain how Central Asian and Iranian culture influenced the Tang dynasty.

2. Describe the city of Chang'an. How was it designed, what were its purposes, and who lived there?

3. Discuss the legacy of the Tang dynasty in China, Japan, and Central Asia.

4. Discuss the process by which Tibet came to be controlled by monks. Why did the same thing not happen in China?

5. Describe Korea's role in the creation of Japanese culture.

6. Describe the rise of the warrior class in Japan. What role did it play?

7. Discuss the role played in China by Champa rice from Annam.

8. Why do women seem to have had more power in South China and Vietnam that in other East Asian countries?

Essay Questions

Make an outline for each question, listing the major points you want to discuss. Then write your practice essay, following your outline carefully and making sure that you do not skip any of your major points. At this time you will want to add the relevant dates and details that will make your essay persuasive and accurate.

1. Discuss the cultural, social, political, and economic impact of Buddhism on East Asia, using specific examples from both China and Japan.

2. Give examples showing that Central Asia was the crossroads of trade. What governments and institutions promoted this trade?

3. Discuss how China, India, Central Asia, Rome, Greece, and the Middle East all influenced Tibet.

4. Discuss the various ways in which China influenced the rest of East Asia. In what ways did Korea, Japan, and Vietnam remain culturally distinct?

5. Compare and contrast the roles and status of men and women in Song dynasty China. Be sure to consider men and women of all classes.

Comparison Charts

Using information gathered from the text, fill in the blank areas of each chart with the relevant data pertaining to the regions and categories listed. (Not all blank areas will necessarily be used.)

Chart 11.1
TWO APPROACHES

	Dates	Social Structure	Trade and Economy	Military	External Threats	Internal Threats	Status of Women	Religion	Technology
Tang Dynasty									
Song Dynasty									

Chart 11.2
CHINA, CENTRAL ASIA, KOREA, JAPAN, AND ANNAM

	Political Structure	Social Structure	Examination System	Confucianism	Buddhism	Status of Women	Economy and Trade	Technology
China								
Central Asia								
Korea								
Japan								
Annam								

Society and Culture

After reading "Society and Culture: Poverty on the Land" in your text, answer the following additional questions.

How could the government have alleviated the destitution of the common people? Would the gentry support all actions the government might take? Why or why not?

Internet Assignment

Keywords: "Buddhist caves"

"Tale of Genji"

Much of the art in the Buddhist caves of western China dates from about the time that the *Tale of Genji* was written. Use the keywords above to find web sites on Buddhist caves and the *Tale of Genji*. You might want to consult the *History WIRED* image library on the Bulliet, *The Earth and Its Peoples* web site (refer to the preface of this study guide for information on how to locate the Bulliet home page).

If you examine the artistic styles of the caves and the *Tale of Genji*, you will notice some similarities. What could account for that? What do these pieces of art demonstrate about the societies that created them? How are the Buddhist caves of China and the *Tale of Genji* useful to modern scholars?

Internet Exploration

Poetry was always considered the perfect literary form in China, and it was during the Tang dynasty that poetry reached its peak. One of the most beloved poets of the day was Li Bai (also known as Li Bo and Li Po). Use the keywords "Li Bai" to find some examples of his poetry. One site you may enjoy is www.chinapage.com/libai2n.html. Many of these sites have audio, Chinese characters, and all have English translations. What kinds of things did Li Bai write about? Is his poetry still relevant today?

Map Exercise

On Outline Map 11.1, mark the extent of these empires:

Tang Empire
Song Empire
Liao Empire

Uigur Empire
Southern Song
Jin Empire

Then plot the location of the following:

Chang'an (Xi'an)
Sogdiana
Ferghana

Transoxiana
Dunhuang
Silla

Outline Map 11.1

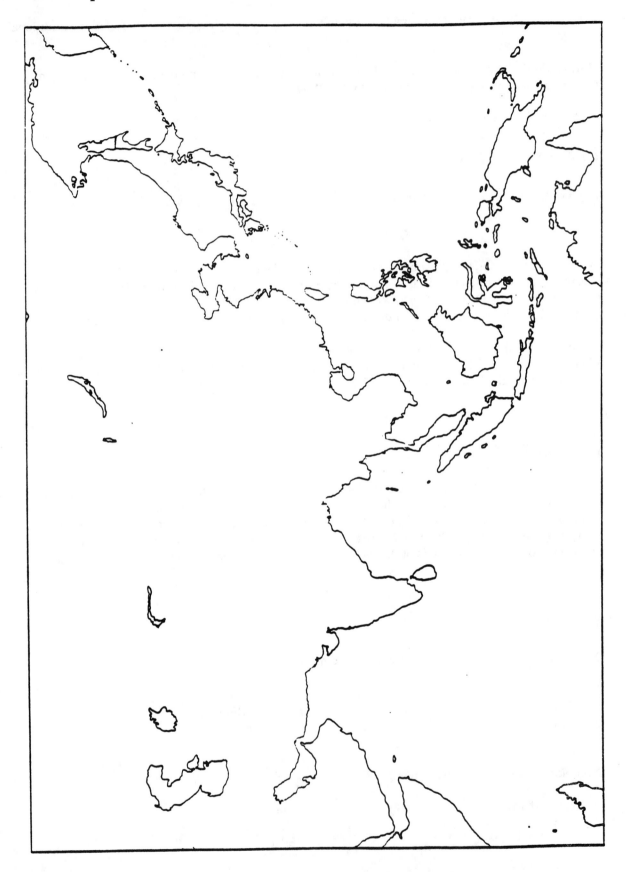

CHAPTER 12

Peoples and Civilizations of the Americas, 200–1500 C.E.

Learning Objectives

After reading Chapter 12 and completing this study chapter, you should be able to explain:

- How isolation from other continents shaped technological and social developments in the Americas.

- How each region of the Americas differed geographically, and how these differences influenced the development of the diverse cultures of the Americas.

- What environmental challenges the peoples of the Americas faced, and how they met those challenges.

- How the cultural legacies of early cultures such as the Olmec and Chavín civilizations shaped the societies that followed them, and why the cultural traditions of the Americas proved very durable.

Chapter Outline

In the outline below, include important themes, concepts, and details in the blank spaces provided. If you find fewer points than you have space for, leave lines blank. If you find more points, add as many lines as necessary.

I. Introduction

    A. *The marriage alliance between Dos Pilas and Naranjo*

        1. _____

        2. _____

        3. _____

B. <u>*Scarce resources, warfare, and dynastic crisis*</u>

    1. _____

    2. _____

    3. _____

C. <u>*Cultural diversity resulted in many different political and technological solutions*</u>

    1. _____

    2. _____

    3. _____

II. **Classic-Era Culture and Society in Mesoamerica, 200–900**

A. <u>*Teotihuacan*</u>

    1. <u>*Religion*</u>

        a. _____

        b. _____

        c. _____

    2. <u>*Population growth and agriculture*</u>

        a. _____

        b. _____

        c. _____

    3. <u>*Administration and commercial interests*</u>

        a. _____

        b. _____

        c. _____

        d. _____

        e. _____

      f. _____

4. *Military* _____

      a. _____

      b. _____

      c. _____

5. *Decline* _____

      a. _____

      b. _____

      c. _____

      d. _____

B. *The Maya* _____

1. *Agriculture* _____

      a. _____

      b. _____

      c. _____

      d. _____

2. *City states and systems of control* _____

      a. _____

      b. _____

      c. _____

      d. _____

      e. _____

3. *Religious cosmology* _____

    a. _____

    b. _____

    c. _____

4. *Rulers and warfare* _____

    a. _____

    b. _____

    c. _____

    d. _____

    e. _____

5. *Bloodletting and lineage* _____

    a. _____

    b. _____

    c. _____

    d. _____

6. *Technology—particularly the calendar* _____

    a. _____

    b. _____

    c. _____

    d. _____

    e. _____

    f. _____

7. *Decline of Maya centers* _____

    a. _____

    b. _____

c. _____

d. _____

III. The Post-Classic Period in Mesoamerica, 900–1500

A. *The Toltecs* _____

   1. *Borrowed and built on earlier societies* _____

     a. _____

     b. _____

     c. _____

   2. *Most important innovations were political and military* _____

     a. _____

     b. _____

     c. _____

     d. _____

   3. *Rule of Tula* _____

     a. _____

     b. _____

     c. _____

   4. *Decline* _____

     a. _____

     b. _____

     c. _____

B. *The Aztecs* _____

   1. *Early relations with urbanized agriculturalists and military conquest* _____

     a. _____

b. _____

c. _____

2. *Expansion and rulers* _____

   a. _____

   b. _____

   c. _____

3. *Military expansion and clan influence* _____

   a. _____

   b. _____

   c. _____

4. *Government legitimacy through ritual and class divisions* ___

   a. _____

   b. _____

   c. _____

   d. _____

   e. _____

5. *Food production and acquisition* _____

   a. _____

   b. _____

   c. _____

   d. _____

   e. _____

6. *Commerce and markets* _____

a. _____

b. _____

c. _____

d. _____

e. _____

7. *Religion and human sacrifice* _____

    a. _____

    b. _____

    c. _____

    d. _____

    e. _____

    f. _____

V. Northern Peoples

A. *The Southwestern Desert Cultures* _____

    1. *The Hohokam* _____

        a. _____

        b. _____

        c. _____

        d. _____

    2. *Anasazi economy, products, and kivas* _____

        a. _____

        b. _____

        c. _____

    3. *Structure of Chaco Canyon towns and society* _____

a. _____

b. _____

c. _____

d. _____

4.   *Political and religious dominance in Chaco Canyon and trade* _____

    a. _____

    b. _____

    c. _____

    d. _____

    e. _____

    f. _____

5.   *The abandonment of Chaco Canyon* _____

    a. _____

    b. _____

    c. _____

    d. _____

B.   *The Mound Builders: The Adena, Hopewell, and Mississippian Cultures* _____

1.   *Adena people of the Ohio Valley* _____

    a. _____

    b. _____

    c. _____

2.   *Hopewell culture* _____

    a. _____

    b. _____

        c. _____

        d. _____

        e. _____

    3. *Mississippian culture* _____

        a. _____

        b. _____

        c. _____

        d. _____

    4. *Cahokia* _____

        a. _____

        b. _____

        c. _____

        d. _____

        e. _____

    5. *Decline of Cahokia* _____

        a. _____

        b. _____

        c. _____

VI. **Andean Civilizations, 200–1500**

  A. *Cultural Response to Environmental Challenge* _____

    1. *Record keeping and reciprocal obligations* _____

        a. _____

        b. _____

        c. _____

2. *Large-scale organization of labor and gendered division of tasks*

    a. _____

    b. _____

    c. _____

3. *Exploitation of the environment and colonizing*

    a. _____

    b. _____

    c. _____

B. *Moche and Chimú*

1. *Moche regional control and production*

    a. _____

    b. _____

    c. _____

    d. _____

    e. _____

2. *Moche society highly stratified and theocratic*

    a. _____

    b. _____

    c. _____

    d. _____

    e. _____

    f. _____

3. *High-quality artisans and art*

a. _____

b. _____

c. _____

d. _____

4. *Decline of the Moche* _____

   a. _____

   b. _____

   c. _____

   d. _____

   e. _____

C. *Tiwanaku and Wari* _____

1. *Tiwanaku: agriculture and architecture* _____

   a. _____

   b. _____

   c. _____

   d. _____

2. *Tiwanaku: social structure and trade* _____

   a. _____

   b. _____

   c. _____

   d. _____

3. *Influence of Tiwanaku* _____

   a. _____

   b. _____

c. _____

4. *Wari* _____

    a. _____

    b. _____

    c. _____

    d. _____

    e. _____

    f. _____

D. *The Inca* _____

1. *The rise of the Inca state and conquest* _____

    a. _____

    b. _____

    c. _____

    d. _____

    e. _____

2. *Pastoralism and the state labor system* _____

    a. _____

    b. _____

    c. _____

    d. _____

    e. _____

    f. _____

3. *Imperial administration* _____

a. _____

b. _____

c. _____

d. _____

e. _____

4. *Urban design and the building of Cuzco* _____

a. _____

b. _____

c. _____

d. _____

e. _____

5. *Inca cultural and technological achievements rest on earlier Andean civilizations* _____

a. _____

b. _____

c. _____

d. _____

e. _____

f. _____

6. *Decline* _____

a. _____

b. _____

c. _____

d. _____

VII. Conclusion

    A. *Environmental role in rise of American societies* _____

        1. _____

        2. _____

        3. _____

    B. *Culmination of American process in Aztec and Inca Empires* _____

        1. _____

        2. _____

        3. _____

    C. *Military, commerce, and the exploitation of people* _____

        1. _____

        2. _____

        3. _____

    D. *An end to isolation* _____

        1. _____

        2. _____

        3. _____

Identifications

Define each term and explain why it is significant, including any important dates.

	Identification	*Significance*
maize		
bloodletting rituals		
Teotihuacan		

	Identification	*Significance*
chinampas		
Maya		
Toltecs		
Aztecs		
Tenochtitlan		
tribute system		
Huitzilopochtli		
Anasazi		
chiefdom		
khipu		
ayllu		
mit'a		
Moche		
llamas and alpacas		
Chimú		
coca		
Tiwanaku		

	Identification	*Significance*
Wari		
Inca		
acllas		

Multiple-Choice Questions

Read the entire question, including *all* the possible answers. Then choose the *one* answer that best fits the question.

1. Which of the following staple crops became the most important food crop in the Americas?
   a. Maize
   b. Manioc
   c. Sunflowers
   d. Peanuts

2. Which of the following statements best describes Amerindian interaction with the environment?
   a. Amerindians were caretakers and preserved the natural environment.
   b. Amerindians had limited impact on the environment, but it was Europeans who really changed the environment.
   c. Amerindians manipulated the environment to their own ends long before the arrival of Europeans.
   d. Amerindians did more damage to the environment than Europeans.

3. Which of the following indicates that Teotihuacan probably used its military to expand its trade relations?
   a. The discovery of representations of soldiers in Teotihuacan dress in the Maya region of Guatemala
   b. Written accounts by the Maya and Moche
   c. Swords found in graves all over Mesoamerica
   d. Written accounts found in Teotihuacan

4. Typically, Maya military forces fought to secure
   a. trade goods and routes.
   b. captives rather than territory.
   c. territory rather than captives.
   d. territory and important religious sites.

5. Which of the following statements is *not* true about the postclassic period in Mesoamerica?
   a. Population decreased.
   b. Agricultural practices intensified.
   c. Many rulers increased the size of their armies.
   d. Rulers used new political institutions to facilitate their control of diverse peoples and regions.

6. Which group gained land and peasant labor from Aztec military expansion?
   a. The kinship-based clans
   b. The priests
   c. The warrior elite
   d. The peasants

7. Which of the following is *not* true of the Toltecs?
   a. They created the first conquest state based largely on military power.
   b. Unlike earlier Mesoamerican societies, they never practiced human sacrifice.
   c. The Aztecs incorrectly believed that they were the source of nearly all of the cultural achievements of the Mesoamerican world.
   d. Their use of two chieftans eventually weakened the state.

8. What is the most likely reason that the sites in Chaco Canyon were abandoned by the Anasazi?
   a. Warfare with the neighboring Hohokam, Sinagua, and Hopi
   b. Bubonic plague
   c. A long drought, which undermined the agricultural economy
   d. The migratory habits of the Anasazi, who moved several times a year

9. What is the most likely explanation for the Hopewell culture possessing the knowledge to grow maize, squash, and beans?
   a. They got it from Mesoamerican cultures.
   b. They developed it on their own.
   c. They learned it from the Anasazi.
   d. They learned it from contact with cultures living between them and Mesoamerica.

10. Unique environmental challenges led to especially distinctive highland and coastal cultures in
    a. the Andes.
    b. Mesoamerica.
    c. Chaco Canyon.
    d. the Ohio Valley.

11. The Inca civilization was originally based on
    a. control of religious institutions.
    b. military dominance.
    c. reciprocal gift giving and the redistribution of textiles.
    d. the control of jade, like the Olmec civilization.

12. The Inca conquest of large populations in environmentally distinct regions permitted economic growth, but
    a. the population decreased.
    b. it increased warfare with Mesoamerica.
    c. it caused eventual economic decline.
    d. it reduced equality among people.

13. All scholars agree that the cultural center of Wari
    a. was a dependency of Tiwanaku.
    b. was a twin capital of Tiwanaku.
    c. was most closely related to the Moche.
    d. scholars do not agree, as there are many, as yet unproven, viable theories.

14. Inca prosperity and military strength depended on
    a. human sacrifice.
    b. llamas and alpacas.
    c. khipus.
    e. agriculture.

Short-Answer Questions

Answer each question in one short paragraph, giving the definition, dates, and significance.

1. How did Amerindians alter the landscape and why?

2. If Teotihuacan did not have a single strong ruler, how then was the state controlled?

3. Discuss the role of religion in Maya culture.

4. What are the different theories explaining the decline of Maya civilization? What kind of evidence is there to support these theories?

5. Describe three water-control and irrigation projects undertaken by Americans.

6. Why did Americans practice human sacrifice? Was it practiced more by one group than another, and if so, why?

7. How did the Inca ensure that leaving defeated local leaders in power would succeed?

Essay Questions

Make an outline for each question, listing the major points you want to discuss. Then write your practice essay, following your outline carefully and making sure that you do not skip any of your major points. At this time you will want to add the relevant dates and details that will make your essay persuasive and accurate.

1. Discuss the similarities that united the cultures of Mesoamerica. What divided them?

2. Compare and contrast the roles of women in at least three American societies.

3. What environmental challenges faced the peoples of the Americas? How did they cope with these challenges? Choose examples from three cultures.

4. Discuss cultural sharing, influence, and legacies among the peoples of the Americas. Use at least three examples.

5. Trace the rise and fall of two American cultures. What factors led to their initial success, how did they maintain power, and what led to their eventual demise?

6. Compare and contrast two North American cultures (excluding Mesoamerica). What were their political institutions, how did they provide food for their people, and what was their daily lifestyle?

Comparison Charts

Using information gathered from the text, fill in the blank areas of each chart with the relevant data pertaining to the regions and categories listed. (Not all blank areas will necessarily be used.)

Chart 12.1
AMERICAN TECHNOLOGY

	Agriculture/ Migration/ Flood Control	Mathematics/ Astronomy	Art/Architecture Urban Planning	Economics/ Trade	Population Control	Politics
Teotihuacan						
Maya						
Aztecs						
Anasazi						
Hopewell/ Mississippian						
Moche						
Tiwanaku						
Inca						

Chart 12.2
THE AZTECS AND THE INCA

	Region/Dates	Rise	Political System	Social Features	Internal and External Relations	Decline
Aztecs						
Inca						

Society and Culture

After reading "Society and Culture: Acllas" in your text, answer the following additional questions.

Why do you think that it was necessary for acllas to be virgins? What benefits might have been experienced by the families of the acllas?

Internet Assignment

Keywords: "Machu Picchu"

"Mesa Verde"

Both Machu Picchu and Mesa Verde were built by peoples belonging to sophisticated cultures. Use the above keywords to find web sites about these structures. You might want to consult the *History WIRED* image library on the Bulliet, *The Earth and Its Peoples* web site (refer to the preface of this study guide for information on how to locate the Bulliet home page).

Though the societies themselves appear to have been quite different, Machu Picchu and Mesa Verde are very similar. Why? What may have motivated their builders' site selection? What are the two structures made of, and why? What may account for their different preservation rates?

Internet Exploration

Today many people find the taste of chocolate divine, but did you know that to the ancient Maya and Aztecs chocolate *was* divine? Try the keywords "Mexico and Xocoatl" or "Xocoatl and Mexico" to learn more about this sacred substance. Two specific web sites you might enjoy are: http://mexsa.com/coin2.htm and http://www.mythinglinks.org/ip~cacao.html. Who brought chocolate to the ancient Mexicans? What were chocolate's ritual purposes?

Map Exercise

On Outline Map 12.1, mark the extent of the following:

Maya civilization, 150 B.C.E.–900 C.E.

Aztec Empire, 1519 C.E.

Anasazi culture

Mound-building cultures

Mochica state, 200–700 C.E.

Inca Empire, 1532 C. E.

Then plot the following:

Tenochtitlan

Tikal

Tulum

Chichén Itza

Cuzco

Lake Titicaca

Outline Map 12.1

CHAPTER 13

Western Eurasia, 1200–1500

Learning Objectives

After reading Chapter 13 and completing this study chapter, you should be able to explain:

- How the Mongols united under Genghis Khan, and what factors particular to Central Asia contributed to their rise.

- How the Mongols dominated large regions of western Eurasia, and what their long-term impact was, including facilitating the rise of nationalism, creating new, wealthy urban centers, and impoverishing the countryside.

- In what ways Mongol control made East-West contact easier, bringing new ideas, goods, people, and diseases.

- What impact Islam had on the politics, arts, literature, and intellectual movements in Central Asia, the Middle East, and Europe.

Chapter Outline

In the outline below, include important themes, concepts, and details in the blank spaces provided. If you find fewer points than you have space for, leave lines blank. If you find more points, add as many lines as necessary.

   I. **Introduction**

       A. *Temujin* _____

           1. _____

           2. _____

           3. _____

B. *Genghis Khan* _____

    1. _____

    2. _____

    3. _____

C. *The common view of the Mongols* _____

    1. _____

    2. _____

    3. _____

D. *Mongol legacies* _____

    1. _____

    2. _____

    3. _____

    4. _____

    5. _____

II. **The Rise of the Mongols, 1200–1260**

A. *Nomadism in Central Asia* _____

    1. *Nomadism* _____

        a. _____

        b. _____

        c. _____

    2. *Centralized decision making* _____

        a. _____

        b. _____

        c. _____

3. *Competition for resources and slavery*

    a. _____

    b. _____

    c. _____

4. *Religion*

    a. _____

    b. _____

    c. _____

5. *Self-sufficiency and iron*

    a. _____

    b. _____

    c. _____

    d. _____

    e. _____

    f. _____

B. *The Mongol Conquests*

1. *Early conquests and khans*

    a. _____

    b. _____

    c. _____

    d. _____

    e. _____

    f. _____

2. *How did such a small group of people conquer such a large land mass?*

    a. _____

    b. _____

    c. _____

3. *The advantages of surrender*

    a. _____

    b. _____

    c. _____

    d. _____

    e. _____

    f. _____

C. *Overland Trade and the Plague*

1. *Silk and trade*

    a. _____

    b. _____

    c. _____

2. *Travelers' accounts*

    a. _____

    b. _____

    c. _____

3. *Mongol policy affected Christian-Muslim relations*

    a. _____

    b. _____

c. _____

4. *The bubonic plague* _____

   a. _____

   b. _____

   c. _____

III. **The Fall and Rise of Islam, 1260–1500**

   A. *Mongol Rivalry* _____

   1. *The choice between Buddhism and Islam* _____

      a. _____

      b. _____

      c. _____

   2. *Conflicts between Muslims and Mongols* _____

      a. _____

      b. _____

      c. _____

      d. _____

      e. _____

      f. _____

   3. *Il-khans and Crusaders* _____

      a. _____

      b. _____

      c. _____

      d. _____

      e. _____

      f. _____

B. *Muslims and the State* _____

    1. *The Il-khans and taxation* _____

       a. _____

       b. _____

       c. _____

    2. *Economic troubles and Ghazan* _____

       a. _____

       b. _____

       c. _____

    3. *Power in Russia weakens* _____

       a. _____

       b. _____

       c. _____

C. *Art and Science in Islamic Eurasia* _____

    1. *Brilliant period in Islamic civilization—great influence on Europe and transmitter of ideas from China* _____

       a. _____

       b. _____

       c. _____

       d. _____

       e. _____

       f. _____

    2. *Juvaini's work and influence* _____

a. _____

b. _____

c. _____

d. _____

e. _____

f. _____

3. _Rashid al-Din and Ibn Khaldun_ _____

a. _____

b. _____

c. _____

d. _____

e. _____

f. _____

4. _Nasir al-Din Tusi_ _____

a. _____

b. _____

c. _____

d. _____

e. _____

f. _____

5. _Il-khans and astronomy_ _____

a. _____

b. _____

c. _____

d. _____

e. _____

f. _____

IV. Regional Definition in Response to the Mongols

A. *Russia and Rule from Afar* _____

1. *Mongol conquests in Russia* _____

a. _____

b. _____

c. _____

d. _____

e. _____

f. _____

2. *Mongol effects on Russian culture* _____

a. _____

b. _____

c. _____

d. _____

e. _____

f. _____

3. *Mongol effects on Russian politics* _____

a. _____

b. _____

c. _____

B.　*Social Change and Centralization in Europe and Anatolia*

　　1.　*The Teutonic Knights*

　　　　a.　＿＿＿＿＿＿＿＿＿＿＿＿＿＿＿＿＿＿＿＿＿＿＿＿＿＿

　　　　b.　＿＿＿＿＿＿＿＿＿＿＿＿＿＿＿＿＿＿＿＿＿＿＿＿＿＿

　　　　c.　＿＿＿＿＿＿＿＿＿＿＿＿＿＿＿＿＿＿＿＿＿＿＿＿＿＿

　　2.　*Eastern Europe under assault*

　　　　a.　＿＿＿＿＿＿＿＿＿＿＿＿＿＿＿＿＿＿＿＿＿＿＿＿＿＿

　　　　b.　＿＿＿＿＿＿＿＿＿＿＿＿＿＿＿＿＿＿＿＿＿＿＿＿＿＿

　　　　c.　＿＿＿＿＿＿＿＿＿＿＿＿＿＿＿＿＿＿＿＿＿＿＿＿＿＿

　　3.　*Withdrawal of the Mongols and diplomatic relations*

　　　　a.　＿＿＿＿＿＿＿＿＿＿＿＿＿＿＿＿＿＿＿＿＿＿＿＿＿＿

　　　　b.　＿＿＿＿＿＿＿＿＿＿＿＿＿＿＿＿＿＿＿＿＿＿＿＿＿＿

　　　　c.　＿＿＿＿＿＿＿＿＿＿＿＿＿＿＿＿＿＿＿＿＿＿＿＿＿＿

C.　*Stabilization of Mamluk Rule in Egypt*

　　1.　*Thrived while resisting the Mongols*

　　　　a.　＿＿＿＿＿＿＿＿＿＿＿＿＿＿＿＿＿＿＿＿＿＿＿＿＿＿

　　　　b.　＿＿＿＿＿＿＿＿＿＿＿＿＿＿＿＿＿＿＿＿＿＿＿＿＿＿

　　　　c.　＿＿＿＿＿＿＿＿＿＿＿＿＿＿＿＿＿＿＿＿＿＿＿＿＿＿

　　2.　*Mamluk society*

　　　　a.　＿＿＿＿＿＿＿＿＿＿＿＿＿＿＿＿＿＿＿＿＿＿＿＿＿＿

　　　　b.　＿＿＿＿＿＿＿＿＿＿＿＿＿＿＿＿＿＿＿＿＿＿＿＿＿＿

　　　　c.　＿＿＿＿＿＿＿＿＿＿＿＿＿＿＿＿＿＿＿＿＿＿＿＿＿＿

　　3.　*Trade and the plague*

a. _____

b. _____

c. _____

V. Conclusion

A. *Characteristics of Mongol society gave them advantages* _____

   1. _____

   2. _____

   3. _____

B. *Mongol legacy* _____

   1. _____

   2. _____

   3. _____

   4. _____

   5. _____

   6. _____

C. *Effects of the plague* _____

   1. _____

   2. _____

   3. _____

Identifications

Define each term and explain why it is significant, including any important dates.

	Identification	*Significance*
Genghis Khan		
khan		
Mongols		
nomadism		
steppe		
iron		
bubonic plague		
Il-khan		
Golden Horde		
Mongol bow		
Juvaini		
Rashid al-Din		
tax farming		
Ibn Khaldun		
Nasir al-Din Tusi		
"Arabic" numerals		

	Identification	*Significance*
Alexander Nevskii		
Ottomans		
Mamluks		

Multiple-Choice Questions

Read the entire question, including *all* the possible answers. Then choose the *one* answer that best fits the question.

1. The rise of Genghis Khan and the Mongols can be attributed
   a. solely to the charisma and military genius of Genghis Khan.
   b. at least partially to the long-term trends and pressures of Central Asia.
   c. to the lack of competition for resources in Central Asia.
   d. to unusual weather patterns in the twelfth century.

2. Which of the following best describes the religious atmosphere on the steppe?
   a. There was a mix of religious affiliations.
   b. Islam had quickly eroded all other influences.
   c. Buddhism still reigned supreme.
   d. Christianity had begun making significant inroads among the clans.

3. If attacked by the Mongols, what would be the best course of action?
   a. Meet out on the field where the Mongol cavalry was weak.
   b. Open the city gates to fight.
   c. Keep the gates closed, but don't surrender.
   d. Surrender.

4. Which of the following is *not* true?
   a. Europe had not seen any outbreaks of the plague since 700.
   b. The plague had been festering in China since the early years of the Tang dynasty.
   c. The Middle East had not seen any outbreaks of the plague since 1200.
   d. All of Eurasia had suffered a series of plagues throughout the eleventh and twelfth centuries.

5. The plague was brought to Europe in the fourteenth century by
   a. the Mongols.
   b. Tamerlane.
   c. traders.
   d. Crusaders.

6. Why did a diplomatic correspondence occur between Pope Nicholas IV and the Il-khan court?
   a. Pope Nicholas IV hoped to enlist the Il-khans in driving Muslim Mongols from Russia.
   b. Pope Nicholas IV needed to ransom the Christian residents of Jerusalem.
   c. The Il-khans were interested in converting to Christianity to distance themselves from Muslim Mongols.
   d. Physicians on both sides had been requesting diplomatic help to find a cure for the plague.

7. What single event probably prevented Europe from being overrun by Mongol forces in the thirteenth century?
   a. The battle fought at Tours by Charles Martel
   b. The plague
   c. The collapse of the Song dynasty, which caused the Mongols to focus their attention eastward
   d. The death of the Great Khan Ögödei and the necessity to elect his successor

8. The Mongol armies in western Eurasia were made up mostly of
   a. ethnic Mongols.
   b. Uigur mercenaries.
   c. captured Christians.
   d. an international force.

9. What innovation adopted by European scholars from Middle Eastern scholars made possible precise calculations, for instance in astronomy?
   a. "Arabic" numerals from India
   b. The abacus from China
   c. Roman numerals
   d. Greek mathematics

10. To enhance their ability to control Russia, the Mongols
    a. undermined local elites.
    b. converted to Christianity.
    c. promoted farmers to positions of power.
    d. had a partnership with the Russian elites.

11. Frederick II conspired with the Mamluks to give the illusion of having captured Jerusalem because he
    a. was threatened with excommunication by the pope unless he helped in the campaigns to capture religious sites in Palestine and Syria.
    b. was actually preparing for war against the Papal States.
    c. had lost the war and was paying tribute to the Mamluks.
    d. wanted the prestige of capturing the Holy Land so that he might become pope himself.

12. What influenced the rise in the use of vernacular languages in literature in Europe?
    a. The plague
    b. Fashion
    c. The Mongols
    d. The fact that Latin was no longer taught in the schools

13. Which of the following peripheral peoples did not benefit from Mongol control of neighboring lands?
    a. Lithuanians
    b. Russians
    c. the Ottomans
    d. the Mamluks

Short-Answer Questions

Answer each question in one short paragraph, giving the definition, dates, and significance.

1. What lessons did Temüjin learn during his years with the Keraits?

2. Discuss the role of women in Mongol society, and particularly in politics.

3. How did religion in Central Asia support nomadic ideas of rulership? How did it support the Mongols' rise and contribute to their success?

4. What dangers did Islam pose to the Mongol mission in the Middle East?

5. Did Mongol occupation affect the cities and the countryside in the same way? Explain.

6. How did the rule of the Golden Horde differ from that of the Il-khans?

7. What was the overall effect of the Mongol domination on the shaping of Russia?

Essay Questions

Make an outline for each question, listing the major points you want to discuss. Then write your practice essay, following your outline carefully and making sure that you do not skip any of your major points. At this time you will want to add the relevant dates and details that will make your essay persuasive and accurate.

1. Discuss the legacy of the Mongols in western Eurasia. How did they affect the political, economic, religious, and social systems of the peoples they conquered and the peoples they attempted to conquer?

2. Compare and contrast the lifestyles of nomadic and sedentary peoples. How did each earn their livelihood, what was their daily life like, and how did they relate to outside groups?

3. How did the Mongols affect the policies of states in Central Asia and Europe? Give specific examples from at least three countries.

4. Discuss Mongol military technology and governmental techniques. How did the combination of the two bring about the subjugation of most of Eurasia, the control of great masses of people, and the impoverishment of much of the countryside?

5. How did the art, science, and intellectual developments of Islamic Eurasia affect Europe? Use specific examples of each.

Comparison Charts

Using information gathered from the text, fill in the blank areas of each chart with the relevant data pertaining to the regions and categories listed. (Not all blank areas will necessarily be used.)

Chart 13.1
NOMADIC VERSUS SEDENTARY LIFESTYLES

	Geography	Livelihood	Diet	Political Structure	Social Structure	Technology	Population Density	Examples of Peoples
Nomads								
Settled Peoples								

Chart 13.2
MONGOL INFLUENCE ON MONGOL-CONTROLLED TERRITORIES VERSUS PERIPHERAL TERRITORIES

	Rise of Nationalism	Utilization of Technology	Economy and Trade	Religion	Society	Internal Threats	External Threats
Mongol-Controlled Regions							
Peripheral Autonomous Regions							

Society and Culture

After reading "Society and Culture: Dueling Pieties" in your text, answer the following additional questions.

How would Europe have benefited from the conversion of the Great Khan? What would Europe have been like if the Mongols had been able to conquer it?

Internet Assignment

Keywords: **"Genghis Khan"**

"Virtual Mongolia"

Modern day Mongolians have inherited a rich tradition of "world" domination from their Mongol ancestors. Use the above keywords to explore the setting of Genghis Khan's career and compare it to the world of his descendants. You might want to consult the *History WIRED* image library on the Bulliet, *The Earth and Its Peoples* web site (refer to the preface of this study guide for information on how to locate the Bulliet home page).

How are their worlds the same? How are they different? What influence has the environment had on the life of the peoples of the steppe?

Internet Exploration

Yurts (the Mongols called them ger) were the housing option of choice for the Mongols. Use the keyword "yurt" to find some web sites discussing yurts. Two sites you may enjoy are www.nomadicjourneys.com/aboutmong/living.htm and www.woodlandyurts.freeserve.co.uk/ger.htm. Why were yurts so well suited to life on the steppe? What would it be like to live in a yurt? Did you notice any web sites featuring the modern use of yurts? What about yurts would modern industrial people find appealing? Are their reasons the same as the Mongols of Genghis Khan's time?

Map Exercise

On Outline Map 13.1, trace the route of Marco Polo and of the Mongol raids. Then mark the extent of the domain of the following:

Great Khan   Il-khans
Khanate of the Golden Horde
Khanate of Jagadai

Outline Map 13.1

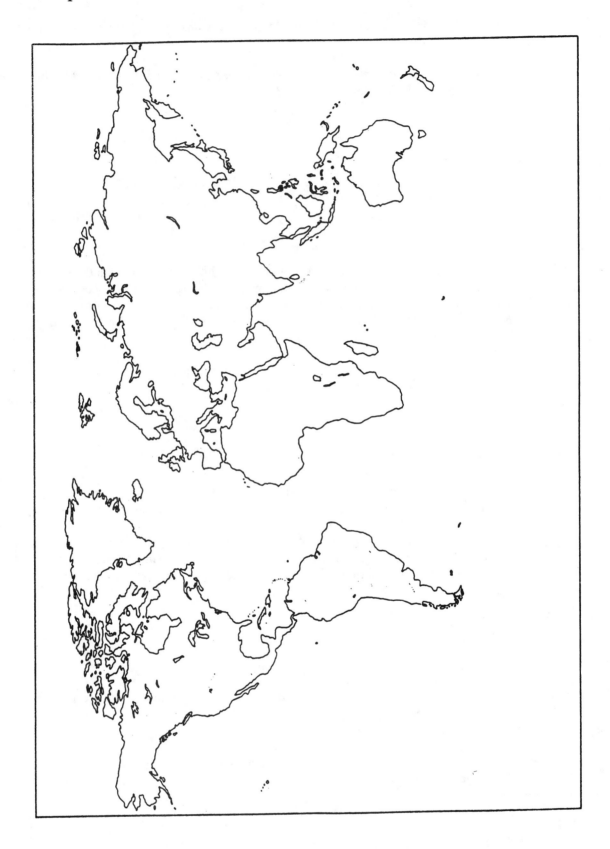

CHAPTER 14

Eastern Eurasia, 1200–1500

Learning Objectives

After reading Chapter 14 and completing this study chapter, you should be able to explain:

- How the land and peoples in eastern Eurasia were influenced by Mongol rule, and in what ways the Mongols' rule in the East compares or contrasts with their rule in the West.

- How the peace imposed by the Mongols helped ideas and technologies pass along trade routes, and how Muslims also participated in that cultural exchange.

- How the Mongols transformed China into a Mongol state, and how the Chinese reacted to that transformation.

- How the Ming Empire addressed the changes wrought by the Mongols.

- How Korea, Japan, and Vietnam developed during the Mongol period, and in what ways Mongol occupation, or the threat of Mongol occupation, influenced their government policies and economic development.

Chapter Outline

In the outline below, include important themes, concepts, and details in the blank spaces provided. If you find fewer points than you have space for, leave lines blank. If you find more points, add as many lines as necessary.

I. Introduction

    A. *Mongol tax system in China*

        1. _____

        2. _____

3. _____

B. *Mongol domination caused various effects in East Asia* _____

1. _____

2. _____

3. _____

C. *Technologies brought by the Mongols* _____

1. _____

2. _____

3. _____

II. **Mongol Domination in Eastern Eurasia, 1200–1368**

A. *The Mongol Conquests, 1206–1279* _____

1. *Eastern conquests and Ögödei* _____

a. _____

b. _____

c. _____

d. _____

e. _____

2. *The selection of the Great Khan* _____

a. _____

b. _____

c. _____

3. *Conflict between Khubilai and Jagadai* _____

a. _____

b. _____

c. _____

d. _____

e. _____

f. _____

4. *Attempted conquests of Vietnam and Java* _____

   a. _____

   b. _____

   c. _____

5. *The selection of the Great Khan* _____

   a. _____

   b. _____

   c. _____

   d. _____

   e. _____

B. *The Yuan Empire, 1279–1368* _____

1. *Chinese influence on Khubilai Khan and the capital at Beijing and Shangdu (Xanadu)* _____

   a. _____

   b. _____

   c. _____

   d. _____

   e. _____

2. *Mongol rule in China* _____

   a. _____

b. _____

c. _____

d. _____

e. _____

f. _____

3. *The ranking of Mongol society* _____

   a. _____

   b. _____

   c. _____

4. *The role of Confucianism in Yüan China* _____

   a. _____

   b. _____

   c. _____

   d. _____

   e. _____

   f. _____

5. *Mongol administration* _____

   a. _____

   b. _____

   c. _____

6. *Economy and merchants* _____

   a. _____

   b. _____

      c. _____

      d. _____

      e. _____

      f. _____

      g. _____

7. *Cottage industries* _____

      a. _____

      b. _____

      c. _____

8. *Rural areas and population decline* _____

      a. _____

      b. _____

      c. _____

      d. _____

      e. _____

      f. _____

D. *Scientific Exchange* _____

1. *Information spread from China to West Asia and back* _____

      a. _____

      b. _____

      c. _____

2. *The Il-Khans imported scholars from China* _____

      a. _____

      b. _____

c. _____

3. *Mixing Chinese and Muslim ideas in math, science, and medicine* _____

a. _____

b. _____

c. _____

E. *Dispersal of the Mongols* _____

1. *Disintegration of the Mongol empire in China* _____

a. _____

b. _____

c. _____

2. *Ming takeover and continuing Mongol influence* _____

a. _____

b. _____

c. _____

d. _____

e. _____

3. *Manchuria and Mongol control* _____

a. _____

b. _____

c. _____

III. **The Early Ming Empire, 1368–1500**

A. *Ming China on a Mongol Foundation* _____

1. *Hung Wu and the foundations of the Ming* _____

a. _____

b. _____

c. _____

d. _____

e. _____

f. _____

2. *Economic revitalization and Zheng He*

    a. _____

    b. _____

    c. _____

    d. _____

    e. _____

    f. _____

    g. _____

    h. _____

3. *Purpose of the voyages and their end*

    a. _____

    b. _____

    c. _____

    d. _____

    e. _____

    f. _____

B. *Technology and Population*

1. *Slowing of technology and lower agricultural productivity*

a. _____

b. _____

c. _____

d. _____

e. _____

f. _____

2. *Shift in career patterns and a labor glut may have contributed* _____

a. _____

b. _____

c. _____

3. *Fear of technology transfer and the technology gap between China and Korea and Japan, and later Europe* _____

a. _____

b. _____

c. _____

C. *The Ming Achievment* _____

1. *Late 1300s and 1400s a time of cultural brilliance* _____

a. _____

b. _____

c. _____

2. *"Plain writing" and two popular works* _____

a. _____

b. _____

c. _____

d. _____

e. _____

f. _____

3. *Advances in porcelain production* _____

    a. _____

    b. _____

    c. _____

IV. **Centralization and Militarism in East Asia, 1200–1500**

    A. *Korea from the Mongols to the Yi, 1231–1500* _____

        1. *Mongol plans for Korea and Korean response* _____

            a. _____

            b. _____

            c. _____

            d. _____

        2. *Mongol effect on Korea and cultural growth* _____

            a. _____

            b. _____

            c. _____

            d. _____

            e. _____

            f. _____

        3. *The fall of Koryo and the rise of the Yi dynasty* _____

            a. _____

            b. _____

c. _____

d. _____

e. _____

f. _____

4.   *Printing and incorporation of Eurasian technology* _____

a. _____

b. _____

c. _____

d. _____

e. _____

f. _____

5.   *Agricultural and military advancements* _____

a. _____

b. _____

c. _____

d. _____

e. _____

f. _____

B.   *Political Transformation in Japan, 1274–1500* _____

1.   *The first Mongol assault on Japan* _____

a. _____

b. _____

c. _____

d. _____

e. _____

f. _____

2. *The Japanese response to the second attack* _____

   a. _____

   b. _____

   c. _____

   d. _____

   e. _____

   f. _____

3. *The Ashikaga Shogunate* _____

   a. _____

   b. _____

   c. _____

   d. _____

   e. _____

   f. _____

C. *The Emergence of Vietnam, 1200–1500* _____

   1. *Mongols in Vietnam* _____

      a. _____

      b. _____

      c. _____

   2. *Conflict between Annam and Champa* _____

      a. _____

        b. _____

        c. _____

    3. *Annam had defeated Champa by 1500*_____

        a. _____

        b. _____

        c. _____

V. Conclusion

   A. *Mongol legacy in China*_____

     1. _____

     2. _____

     3. _____

   B. *Ming*_____

     1. _____

     2. _____

     3. _____

   B. *Mongol legacy in Korea*_____

     1. _____

     2. _____

     3. _____

   D. *Mongol legacy in Japan and Mongol legacy in Vietnam*_____

     1. _____

     2. _____

     3. _____

Identifications

Define each term and explain why it is significant, including any important dates.

	Identification	*Significance*
Ögödei		
Genghis Khan		
Yuan Empire		
lama		
Khubilai Khan		
Beijing		
cottage industries		
Manchuria		
Ming Empire		
Yongle		
Forbidden City		
Zheng He		
technology transfer		
medicine		
Yi		
movable type		

	Identification	*Significance*
cotton		
kamikaze		
Ashikaga shogunate		
Annam		
Champa		

Multiple-Choice Questions

Read the entire question, including *all* the possible answers. Then choose the *one* answer that best fits the question.

1. What did Confucian adviser Yelu Chucai talk Ögödei out of doing?
   a. Turning the rich agricultural land of northern China into pastureland
   b. Defeating southern China
   c. Attacking Japan a third time
   d. Making Buddhism the official religion of China

2. When the Mongols came to Chinese territory in the 1220s, they found
   a. a unified empire capable of resisting attack.
   b. an unsophisticated culture in decline from attacks by the Xiongnu..
   c. no "China" as we think of it today.
   d. the Chinese had fled south to Annam.

3. Which of the following groups convinced Genghis Khan to convert to their religion?
   a. Muslims from western Eurasia
   b. Christians from western Eurasia
   c. Daoists from China
   d. Buddhists from Tibet

4. Starting in the 1400s, the Mongols participated in the Ming tributary system because
   a. they wanted to.
   b. the Ming dynasty made them.
   c. doing so would undermine the power of the Jurchen.
   d. the Chinese held the Great Khan captive.

5. According to Mongol law, the status of people within their realms was based on
   a. individual merit.
   b. military expertise.
   c. where they or their ancestors were born.
   d. their educational level.

6. Which one of the following did *not* upset the Confucians?
    a. The introduction of new technologies from the Middle East
    b. The elevated status of merchants under the Mongols
    c. Mongol encouragement of the study and practice of medicine
    d. The comparatively low status of Confucians in Yuan China

7. The Mongolian-influenced Chinese vernacular language is often called
    a. Uigur.
    b. Mandarin.
    c. Urdu.
    d. Hakka.

8. Which of the following statements best characterizes the Mongol attitude toward farmers?
    a. They hated farming and so did nothing to help farmers.
    b. They saw agriculture only as a way to make money, and so always exploited farmers.
    c. They were nomads and so didn't know about things like dams and dikes.
    d. They tried to protect farmers eventually, but it was too late.

9. The change from Yuan to Ming was
    a. more ideological than structural.
    b. not welcomed by the majority of Chinese.
    c. more structural than ideological.
    d. imperceptible.

10. The Ming Empire addressed the problem of hostile western Mongol control of the overland trade routes by
    a. making war on the Mongols.
    b. sending Zheng He to establish connections by sea.
    c. sending Buddhist missionaries as diplomats to negotiate.
    d. bribing the Mongols.

11. The cession of the Chinese voyages of exploration
    a. did not represent a turning away from the sea.
    b. happened because the government was bankrupt.
    c. occurred at the request of the Great Khan.
    d. occurred because of the public outcry against wasted funds.

12. Though the Ming dynasty is not known for its technological advancement, they did excel in
    a. metallurgy.
    b. porcelain production.
    c. shipbuilding.
    d. firearm production.

13. The Mongol threat that did *not* pull Japan together could be characterized as which of the following?
    a. Alien
    b. Terrifying
    c. Successful
    d. Prolonged

14. The most profound effect of the Mongol Empires was
    a. their facilitation of the formation of new centralized states.
    b. their encouragement of the spread of religion.
    c. the spread of technological knowledge.
    d. the decimation of Eurasia.

15. Anecdotal evidence in Chinese records gives the credit for the invention of gunpowder to
    a. Zheng He.
    b. an Indian merchant.
    c. a Sogdian Buddhist monk.
    d. a Korean merchant.

Short-Answer Questions

Answer each question in one short paragraph, giving the definition, dates, and significance.

1. What kind of civil government system did the Mongols use in China, and how did it compare with past Chinese systems?

2. Why did Japanese isolationism during the Mongol period help stabilize China's economy?

3. Why did China suffer such a large population decrease during the Yuan dynasty?

4. Describe some of Korea's and Japan's technological advances during the years 1200 to 1500. Why does their pattern not fit that of China?

5. What was the Mongol impact on Korea and Japan?

6. How did Annam's legal code differ from that of the Ming?

7. Discuss the development and many uses of gunpowder.

Essay Questions

Make an outline for each question, listing the major points you want to discuss. Then write your practice essay, following your outline carefully and making sure that you do not skip any of your major points. At this time you will want to add the relevant dates and details that will make your essay persuasive and accurate.

1. Discuss the legacy of the Mongols in eastern Eurasia. How did they affect the political, economic, religious, and social systems of the peoples they conquered and the peoples they attempted to conquer? Compare and contrast this legacy with the one left by the Mongols in western Eurasia.

2. Why did the Yongle emperor send Zheng He on his voyages of exploration, what did they accomplish, and why were they ended?

3. Discuss the various factors that could have been responsible for the technological slowdown of the Ming dynasty. What effect did the slowdown have on China?

4. Discuss the social, economic, political, and technological developments in Korea under the Yi dynasty.

5. Trace the development of Annam. Consider outside influences, as well as indigenous elements.

Comparison Charts

Using information gathered from the text, fill in the blank areas of each chart with the relevant data pertaining to the regions and categories listed. (Not all blank areas will necessarily be used.)

Chart 14.1
THE MONGOLS IN CHINA

	Land Distribution and Control	Population	Government and Military Organization	Education and Bureaucrats	Economy and Trade	Society and Class	External Relations	Internal Relations	Technology and Science
Pre-Mongol China (Qin, Han, Tang, and Song)									
Yuan Dynasty									
Ming Dynasty									

Chart 14.2
JAPAN

	Dates/ Capital	Government Organization	Technology	Society	Arts	Internal Threats	External Threats	Economy and Trade	Technology and Science
Kamakura Shogunate									
Ashikaga Shogunate									

Society and Culture

After reading "Society and Culture: Everyday Law in Ming China" in your text, answer the following additional questions.

Traditionally the family has been central in Chinese society. With this in mind, what may be responsible for the familial discord present in the law book? Do you think that the Chinese solution to the problem would be the same as the modern American solution?

Internet Assignment

Keywords: "Beijing the Forbidden City"

                   "Zen Gardens"

Architecture is one way that a society expresses itself, and therefore much can be learned about societies from studying art and architecture. Use the above keywords to find web sites about the Forbidden City in China and Japanese Zen gardens. You might want to consult the *History WIRED* image library at the Bulliet, *The Earth and Its Peoples* web site (refer to the preface of this study guide for information on how to locate the Bulliet home page).

When you view pictures of the Forbidden City in China, what kind of culture do you think of? When you look at Japanese Zen gardens, what kind of outlook do you think the people who created it had? Can you find any common ground between the two examples?

Internet Exploration

Most East Asian societies gained the technology of writing from China. Korea too adopted Chinese characters, but the Chinese and Korean languages are quite different, and Chinese characters do not express Korean well. Therefore, a decision was made in Korea to create a better written language. This was a unique development in the history of writing. Use the keyword "han'gul" or visit the sites www.interlog.com/~mmt/Literacy_Book/index.html or http://catcode.com/kintro/index.htm to learn more about written Korean. What is the reason usually given for the development of han'gul? What are some of the controversies surrounding this written language?

Map Exercise

On Outline Map 14.1, trace Zheng He's voyages and mark the extent of the Ming Empire. Then plot these cities:

Beijing   Nanjing
Jingdezhen   Canton

Also mark the following:

Annam
Champa (to 1500)
Yi Korea

Seoul
Kamakura

Outline Map 14.1

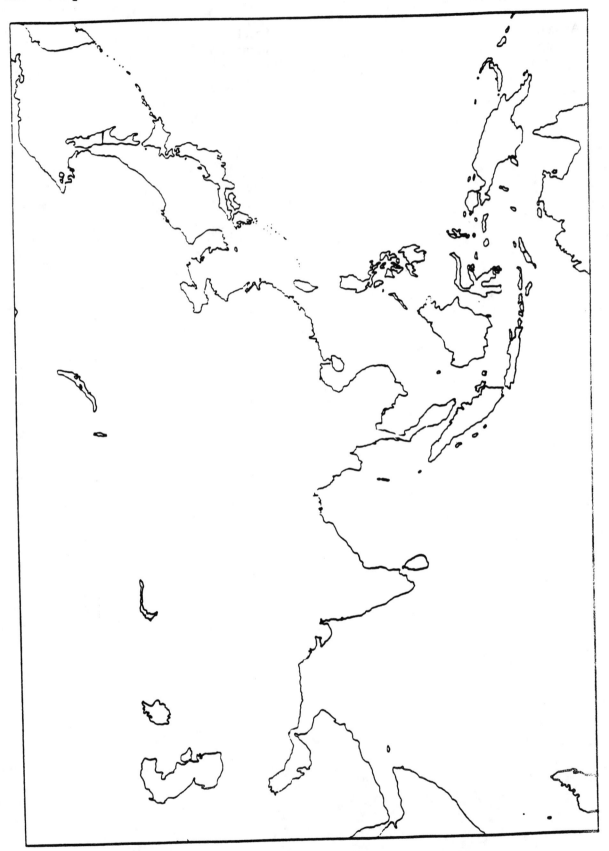

CHAPTER 15

Tropical Africa and Asia, 1200–1500

Learning Objectives

After reading Chapter 15 and completing this study chapter, you should be able to explain:

- How the peoples of the tropics adapted to their environments, what specific techniques or innovations helped them survive, and how certain features of Africa and South Asia united the two regions.

- By what process trade was carried out on the Indian Ocean, who participated, what kind of vessels were used, what goods were exchanged, and who benefited from the system.

- How Islam affected different societies in regard to economics, education, status of women, and architecture.

- In what ways the similarities and differences between the regions of Africa, the Middle East, India, and Southeast Asia affected their political, economic, and social systems, and how the adoption of Islam influenced them differently depending on their circumstances.

Chapter Outline

In the outline below, include important themes, concepts, and details in the blank spaces provided. If you find fewer points than you have space for, leave lines blank. If you find more points, add as many lines as necessary.

I. Introduction

    A. *Ibn Battuta* _____

        1. _____

        2. _____

        3. _____

    B. *Muslim hospitality* _____

1. _____

2. _____

3. _____

C. *Southern Asian and Africa linked geographically and religiously* _____

   1. _____

   2. _____

   3. _____

II. Tropical Lands and Peoples

A. *The Tropical Environment* _____

   1. *Climate—temperature, wind, and rain* _____

      a. _____

      b. _____

      c. _____

      d. _____

      e. _____

   2. *Variations in tropical climates* _____

      a. _____

      b. _____

      c. _____

   3. *Rivers* _____

      a. _____

      b. _____

      c. _____

d. _____

B. *Human Ecosystems* _____

1. *Adapting to natural world fundamental to survival* _____

a. _____

b. _____

c. _____

2. *Some people hunted and gathered their food* _____

a. _____

b. _____

c. _____

d. _____

e. _____

f. _____

3. *Tending herds in arid areas* _____

a. _____

b. _____

c. _____

d. _____

e. _____

f. _____

4. *Farming dominant way of life from 1200 to 1500* _____

a. _____

b. _____

c. _____

    d. _____

    e. _____

5. *Spread of farming and its impact on the environment* _____

    a. _____

    b. _____

    c. _____

C. *Water Systems and Irrigation* _____

1. *Intensive agriculture and irrigation* _____

    a. _____

    b. _____

    c. _____

2. *Delhi Sultanate (1206–1526) and irrigation* _____

    a. _____

    b. _____

    c. _____

3. *Impressive irrigation in Ceylon (Sri Lanka) and Angkor, Cambodia* _____

    a. _____

    b. _____

    c. _____

    d. _____

    e. _____

D. *Mineral Resources* _____

1. *Metal working and iron* _____

a. _____

b. _____

c. _____

2. *Copper* _____

   a. _____

   b. _____

   c. _____

3. *Gold* _____

   a. _____

   b. _____

   c. _____

4. *Connections between metal working and food production* _____

   a. _____

   b. _____

   c. _____

   d. _____

III. New Islamic Empires

  A. *Mali in the Western Sudan* _____

    1. *Spread of Islam through conquest and peacefully* _____

      a. _____

      b. _____

      c. _____

    2. *The rise of Mali* _____

      a. _____

b. _____

c. _____

3. *Mansa Kankan Musa* _____

    a. _____

    b. _____

    c. _____

    d. _____

    e. _____

    f. _____

4. *Fall of Mali* _____

    a. _____

    b. _____

    c. _____

    d. _____

    e. _____

    f. _____

B. *The Delhi Sultanate in India* _____

1. *Islam had a violent arrival* _____

    a. _____

    b. _____

    c. _____

    d. _____

    e. _____

f. _____

2. *Expansion of Muslim rule and a female sultan* _____

   a. _____

   b. _____

   c. _____

   d. _____

   e. _____

   f. _____

   g. _____

3. *Ruthless policies and cruel rulers* _____

   a. _____

   b. _____

   c. _____

4. *Conflict between Hindus and Muslims* _____

   a. _____

   b. _____

   c. _____

   d. _____

   e. _____

5. *Decline of the Delhi Sultanate* _____

   a. _____

   b. _____

   c. _____

   d. _____

e. _____

IV. Indian Ocean Trade

A. *Monsoon Mariners* _____

1. *When Mongol Empire fell ocean route became more important* _____

a. _____

b. _____

c. _____

2. *The dhow was the ship of the Arabian Sea* _____

a. _____

b. _____

c. _____

3. *The junk was the most advanced ship of its day* _____

a. _____

b. _____

c. _____

4. *Trade was decentralized and cooperative* _____

a. _____

b. _____

c. _____

B. *Africa: The Swahili Coast and Zimbabwe* _____

1. *The development of the Swahili language and towns* _____

a. _____

b. _____

　　　c. _____

　2.　*The commercial expansion of Swahili* _____

　　　a. _____

　　　b. _____

　　　c. _____

　3.　*The Great Zimbabwe* _____

　　　a. _____

　　　b. _____

　　　c. _____

C.　*Arabia: Aden and the Red Sea* _____

　1.　*The double blessing of rainfall and location* _____

　　　a. _____

　　　b. _____

　　　c. _____

　2.　*Common commercial interests generally promoted good relations among religion*

　　　a. _____

　　　b. _____

　　　c. _____

　3.　*Conflict over the building of a mosque in Zeila* _____

　　　a. _____

　　　b. _____

　　　c. _____

D.　*India: Gujarat and the Malabar Coast* _____

　1.　*Trade fortunes linked to politics* _____

a. _____

b. _____

c. _____

2. *Exports* _____

a. _____

b. _____

c. _____

3. *Manufacturing* _____

a. _____

b. _____

c. _____

4. *The Malabar Coast* _____

a. _____

b. _____

c. _____

E. *Southeast Asia: The Rise of Malacca* _____

1. *Competition for control over the Straits of Malacca* _____

a. _____

b. _____

c. _____

2. *Rise of a new port at Malacca* _____

a. _____

b. _____

c. _____

3. *An emporium for Southeast Asian trade* _____

a. _____

b. _____

c. _____

V. Social and Cultural Change

A. *Architecture, Learning, and Religion* _____

1. *Architecture and culture* _____

a. _____

b. _____

c. _____

2. *Literacy, education, and Islam* _____

a. _____

b. _____

c. _____

3. *How Islam spread and the results* _____

a. _____

b. _____

c. _____

B. *Social and Gender Distinctions* _____

1. *Growth in slavery accompanied the rising prosperity of the elites* _____

a. _____

b. _____

c. _____

d. _____

e. _____

f. _____

g. _____

2. *Status of tropical women* _____

    a. _____

    b. _____

    c. _____

    d. _____

    e. _____

    f. _____

3. *How did the spread of Islam affect the status of women?* _____

    a. _____

    b. _____

    c. _____

VI. **Conclusion**

    A. *Between 1200 and 1500 the peoples of tropical Africa and Asia drawn closer* _____

        1. _____

        2. _____

        3. _____

    B. *Social and cultural stability—especially at the village level* _____

        1. _____

        2. _____

3. _____

C. *Contrast with events in the Latin West* _____

    1. _____

    2. _____

    3. _____

Identifications

Define each term and explain why it is significant, including any important dates.

                                   Identification   *Significance*

tropics

Ibn Battuta

monsoon

Delhi Sultanate

hunting, fishing, and gathering

farming

gold

Mali

Delhi

Mansa Kankan Musa

Gujarat

Raziya

	Identification	*Significance*
dhow		
junks		
Swahili Coast		
Great Zimbabwe		
Aden		
Malacca		
Urdu		
Timbuktu		
slaves		

Multiple-Choice Questions

Read the entire question, including *all* the possible answers. Then choose the *one* answer that best fits the question.

1. Which of the following did *not* link the peoples of Africa and southern Asia?
    a. Islam
    b. Language
    c. Trade
    d. Environment

2. The dominant way of life for most tropical peoples between 1200 and 1500 was
    a. food gathering.
    b. animal husbandry.
    c. farming.
    d. trade and commerce.

3. As farming spread in tropical Africa and Asia, it
    a. did not always cause permanent changes in the environment.
    b. always damaged the environment.
    c. always replaced native species with introduced species.
    d. created monocultures.

4. Why did the Chinese send a fleet to the Strait of Malacca in 1407?
   a. To take control of the region from the Kingdom of Siam.
   b. To take control of the region from the Java-based kingdom of Majapahit.
   c. To arrest a band of Chinese pirates who controlled the city of Palembang.
   d. To establish a Chinese outpost there to dominate trade in the region.

5. Why did India have to import gold for jewelry and temple decoration from 1200 to 1500?
   a. It had no gold of its own.
   b. It had exhausted its own gold resources.
   c. So many temples were built that gold mining in India could not keep up with the pace.
   d. It had trade agreements with Africa and Southeast Asia that required these imports in order to correct a trade imbalance.

6. The role of force in spreading Islam south of the Sahara was
   a. limited.
   b. considerable.
   c. encouraged by the Quran.
   d. encouraged by the ulama.

7. Which of the following was *not* a factor in the decline of the Delhi Sultanate?
   a. Rivalries within the Muslim elite
   b. The discontent of the Hindus
   c. Revived Mongol interests
   d. Lack of trade

8. How did the collapse of the Mongol Empire in the fourteenth century affect trade?
   a. The overland trade route grew in importance.
   b. The Indian Ocean trade route grew in importance.
   c. All trade between western and eastern Eurasia stopped.
   d. The collapse of the Mongol Empire did not affect Eurasian trade.

9. The trade on the Indian Ocean was
   a. competitive and divisive.
   b. run by imperial decree.
   c. decentralized and cooperative.
   d. never very important to the economy of the area.

10. Which of the following is *not* true about the trading center at Aden?
    a. It was the crossroads for the overland trade route between western and eastern Eurasia.
    b. It had plenty of drinking water because of the monsoonal rains.
    c. It was a convenient stopover for trade with India, the Persian Gulf, East Africa, and Egypt.
    d. It acted as a warehouse for merchants to sort through goods from one place and then send them to another.

11. Which of the following words is *not* Arabic in origin?
    a. Sahara
    b. Sudan
    c. Silk
    d. Swahili

12. Which of the following groups was most instrumental in the spread of Islam?
    a. Soldiers
    b. Monarchs
    c. Merchants
    d. Peasants

13. Which of the following was *least* responsible for the spread of Islam?
    a. Imperial decree
    b. Marriage
    c. Upheavals that helped to wipe out competing religions
    d. Muslim domination of trade and markets

14. The rising prosperity of the elites resulted in
    a. peace.
    b. an increase in slavery.
    c. a decrease in religious fervor.
    d. inflation.

15. Why, according to historians, has the art of brewing received more attention than other "female" arts, such as culinary skills?
    a. Brewing was also a way to make extra money.
    b. Brewing takes more skill than cooking.
    c. Men tended to be the principal consumers of beer.
    d. Muslims are not allowed to consume alcohol, so its consumption is a sin.

16. Which of the following is *not* characteristic of a dhow?
    a. Lateen sails
    b. Mounted cannon
    c. Sewn hull
    d. A rudder

Short-Answer Questions

Answer each question in one short paragraph, giving the definition, dates, and significance.

1. Compare and contrast the complex irrigation systems constructed by powerful governments with those built by local peoples. Assess the advantages and disadvantages of each.

2. Why did the Hindus resent Muslims in India?

3. What brought prosperity to Great Zimbabwe? What brought decline?

4. Trace the rise of Malacca. What geographic and political factors contributed to it?

5. What affected the status of women in Muslim society?

6. Discuss the adoption and adaptation of Muslim practices by non-Muslim and newly Muslim societies.

Essay Questions

Make an outline for each question, listing the major points you want to discuss. Then write your practice essay, following your outline carefully and making sure that you do not skip any of your major points. At this time you will want to add the relevant dates and details that will make your essay persuasive and accurate.

1. How did the peoples of the tropics adapt to their environments? What specific techniques or innovations helped them survive?

2. Describe the systems of extensive and intensive agriculture. What environmental, technological, and social factors influenced people to choose one system or the other? What advantages and disadvantages did each have?

3. Describe the process by which trade was conducted on the Indian Ocean. Who participated, what kind of vessels were used, what goods were exchanged, and who benefited from the system?

4. Discuss how Islam affected economics, education, status of women, and architecture in the different societies it encountered.

5. The writings of Ibn Battuta have long been valued by historians for their perception, veracity, and appeal. Give some examples of his work and discuss them. Can you think of any disadvantages to using his writing?

Comparison Charts

Using information gathered from the text, fill in the blank areas of each chart with the relevant data pertaining to the regions and categories listed. (Not all blank areas will necessarily be used.)

Chart 15.1
TWO MUSLIM EMPIRES

	Dates	Regions	Founding	Government System	Economy and Trade	Society	Technology	Internal Threats	External Threats	Role of Islam	Decline
Mali											
Delhi											

Chart 15.2
INDIAN OCEAN TRADE NETWORK

	Dates	Trading Partners	Trade Goods	Technology	Resources	Society	Cities/Urban Planning	Religion	Decline
Swahili Coast and Zimbabwe									
Arabia: Aden and the Red Sea									
India: Gujarat and the Malabar Coast									
Southeast Asia: The rise of Malacca									

Society and Culture

After reading "Society and Culture: Personal Styles of Rule in India and Mali" in your text, answer the following additional questions.

Can you find evidence of Ibn Battuta's views and opinions in these writings? Which ruler might Ibn Battuta identify with and why?

Internet Assignment

Keywords: "Great Zimbabwe"

                             "Dhow building" or "Arab Dhows"

The culture around the Indian Ocean Trading Basin was quite diverse. Use the above keywords to find web sites about the ruins at Great Zimbabwe and dhow sailing vessels. You might want to consult the *History WIRED* image library on the Bulliet, *The Earth and Its Peoples* web site (refer to the preface of this study guide for information on how to locate the Bulliet home page).

How do the ruins at Great Zimbabwe and the design of the dhow symbolize the cultures of the Indian Ocean peoples? What links the city of Great Zimbabwe and the dhow sailing vessels?

Internet Exploration

Ibn Battuta was a great chronicler of the Muslim world. He traveled far and wide, and kept an interesting record of his experiences. Travel with him by using the keywords "Ibn Battuta" or a site you may enjoy is http://nisus.sfusd.k12.ca.us/schwww/sch618/Ibn_Battuta/Ibn_Battuta_Rihla.html. What was life like on the road? What kinds of places did Ibn Battuta find interesting and how did he view the people he encountered? Do his records have any evidence of how people received him?

Map Exercises

On Outline Map 15.1, mark the wind direction of the two monsoon seasons.

On Outline Map 15.2, mark the following:

Swahili Coast   Timbuktu
Great Zimbabwe   Zeila
Mali
Aden

Then trace the Portuguese routes of exploration and the Muslim trade routes.

On Outline Map 15.3, shade in the extent of the Delhi Sultanate in 1236; the Delhi Sultanate in 1335; and the Delhi Sultanate lands lost in 1335.

On Outline Map 15.4, trace Ibn Battuta's routes. Then mark the extent of these areas:

Majapahit Empire
Islamic world in 850

Lands reconquered by Christian kingdoms
   by 1000
The Islamic world in 1500

Also plot the following:

Malacca
Java

Delhi
Gujarat

Outline Map 15.1

Outline Map 15.2

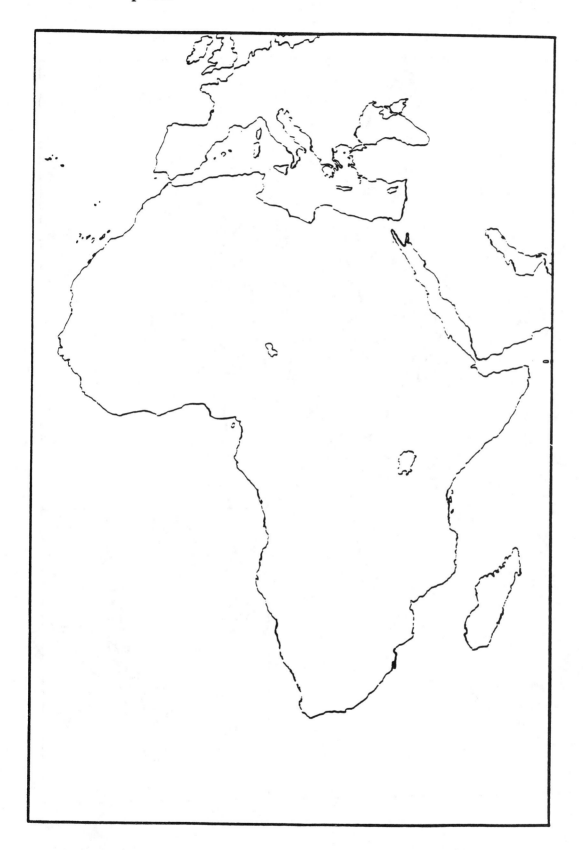

Outline Map 15.3

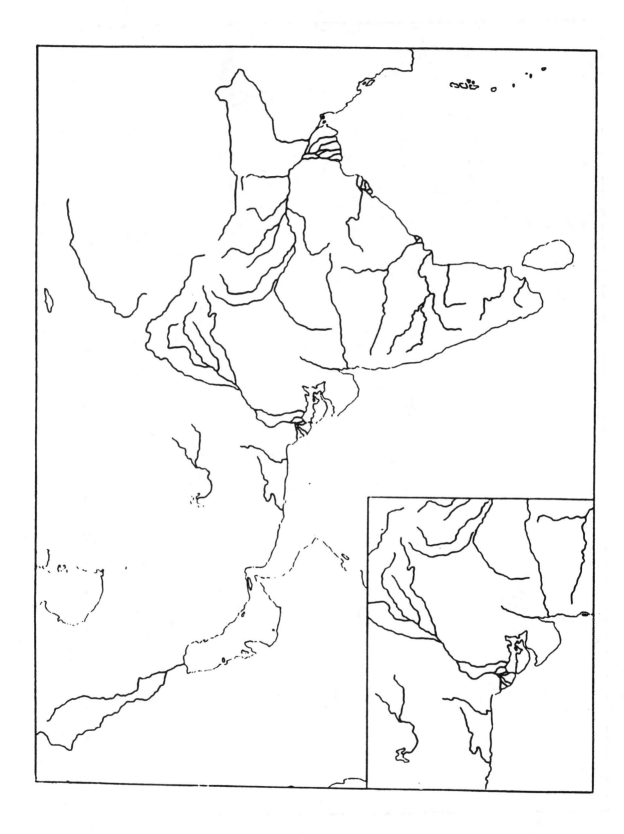

Outline Map 15.4

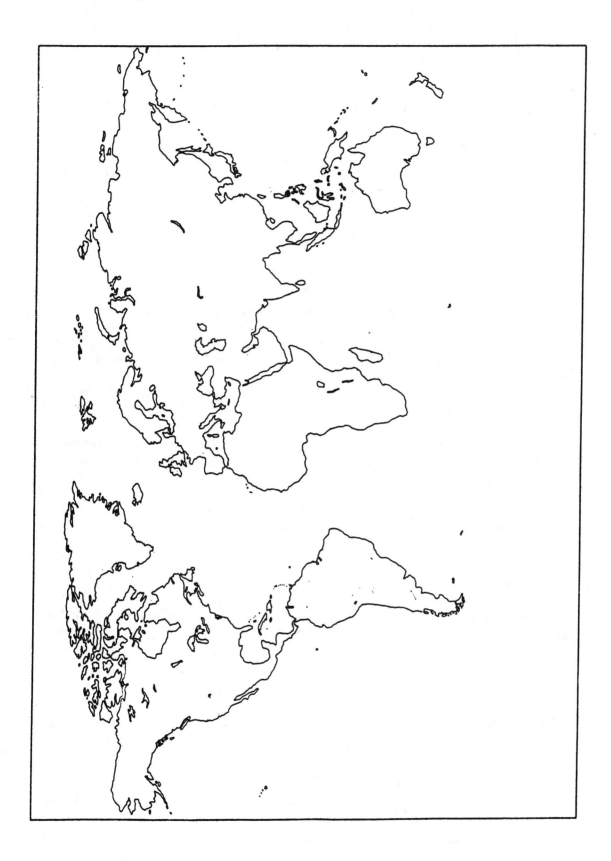

CHAPTER 16

The Latin West, 1200–1500

Learning Objectives

After reading Chapter 16 and completing this study chapter, you should be able to explain:

- How Latin Europe changed during the Late Middle Ages, and how those changes affected the growth of cities, trade, the economy, the status of women, and the use of the environment.

- How Latin Europe began its evolution from a feudal system to a centralized monarchy, and what was involved in this process.

- How the Renaissance grew out of the intellectual milieu of the Middle Ages, how Greco-Roman art and writings preserved by Italy, Byzantium, and the Islamic world influenced it, and in what ways Muslim and Chinese science contributed to the ideas of the Renaissance.

- How the many technological, economic, and social innovations of the Late Middle Ages and the Renaissance in Latin Europe were to change the face of Europe and the world.

Chapter Outline

In the outline below, include important themes, concepts, and details in the blank spaces provided. If you find fewer points than you have space for, leave lines blank. If you find more points, add as many lines as necessary.

I. Introduction

    A. *Lack of European unity* _____

        1. _____

        2. _____

        3. _____

4. _____

5. _____

6. _____

B. *Good and bad aspects of increased prosperity*

   1. _____

   2. _____

   3. _____

C. *Relevance of studying the Latin West*

   1. _____

   2. _____

   3. _____

   4. _____

   5. _____

   6. _____

II. **Rural Growth and Crisis**

A. *Peasants, Population, and Plague*

   1. *Serfs and rural poverty*

      a. _____

      b. _____

      c. _____

      d. _____

      e. _____

      f. _____

   2. *Much needed improvements in agriculture*

a. _____

b. _____

c. _____

d. _____

e. _____

f. _____

3. *The effects of the plague* _____

a. _____

b. _____

c. _____

d. _____

e. _____

f. _____

B. *Social Rebellion* _____

1. *Skilled and manual laborer revolt* _____

a. _____

b. _____

c. _____

2. *The end of serfdom* _____

a. _____

b. _____

c. _____

3. *Urban employers had to raise wages* _____

a. _____

b. _____

c. _____

C. *Mills and Mines* _____

   1. *An early "industrial revolution"?* _____

      a. _____

      b. _____

      c. _____

   2. *Watermills and windmills* _____

      a. _____

      b. _____

      c. _____

      d. _____

      e. _____

      f. _____

   3. *Mining* _____

      a. _____

      b. _____

      c. _____

   4. *Environmental effects* _____

      a. _____

      b. _____

      c. _____

      d. _____

e. _____

f. _____

III. Urban Revival

A. *Trading Cities* _____

1. *Most urban growth in the west after 1200 due to trade and manufacturing* _____

a. _____

b. _____

c. _____

2. *Trade and the "Fourth Crusade" and Marco Polo* _____

a. _____

b. _____

c. _____

d. _____

e. _____

f. _____

3. *The role of the Italian city states in trade* _____

a. _____

b. _____

c. _____

d. _____

e. _____

f. _____

4. *Hanseatic League and other trading centers* _____

a. _____

b. _____

c. _____

d. _____

e. _____

f. _____

5. *Textiles and manufacture* _____

a. _____

b. _____

c. _____

d. _____

e. _____

f. _____

B. *Civic Life* _____

1. *Cities were places of freedom and autonomy* _____

a. _____

b. _____

c. _____

2. *The role of Jews and persecutions* _____

a. _____

b. _____

c. _____

d. _____

e. _____

3. *Guilds: associations for craft specialists* _____

   a. _____

   b. _____

   c. _____

4. *Banking* _____

   a. _____

   b. _____

   c. _____

   d. _____

   e. _____

   f. _____

   g. _____

   h. _____

5. *Usury and Jews* _____

   a. _____

   b. _____

   c. _____

   d. _____

C. *Gothic Cathedrals* _____

1. *Cities built them to compete with each other* _____

   a. _____

   b. _____

   c. _____

2. *Distinctive features* _____

    a. _____

    b. _____

    c. _____

3. *Built by people of practical experience* _____

    a. _____

    b. _____

    c. _____

IV. **Learning, Literature, and the Renaissance**

  A. *Universities and Scholarship* _____

    1. *Availability of Greek and Arab manuscripts* _____

      a. _____

      b. _____

      c. _____

    2. *Monasteries were centers of learning in the early Middle Ages* _____

      a. _____

      b. _____

      c. _____

    3. *Universities* _____

      a. _____

      b. _____

      c. _____

      d. _____

      e. _____

f. _____

4. *Theology was the "queen of the sciences"* _____

   a. _____

   b. _____

   c. _____

   d. _____

   e. _____

B. *Humanists and Printers* _____

   1. *Literature in vernacular languages* _____

      a. _____

      b. _____

      c. _____

   2. *The development and impact of humanism* _____

      a. _____

      b. _____

      c. _____

      d. _____

      e. _____

      f. _____

   3. *The impact of printing—Johann Gutenberg* _____

      a. _____

      b. _____

      c. _____

C. *Renaissance Artists* _____

1. *The evolution of Italian painting*

    a. _____

    b. _____

    c. _____

2. *Leonardo da Vinci (1452–1519) and Michelangelo (1472–1564)*

    a. _____

    b. _____

    c. _____

    d. _____

    e. _____

    f. _____

3. *Patronage fostered an artistic blossoming*

    a. _____

    b. _____

    c. _____

V. Political and Military Transformation

A. *Monarchs, Nobles, and the Church*

1. *The relatively weak position of monarchs*

    a. _____

    b. _____

    c. _____

2. *The role of nobles*

    a. _____

b. _____

c. _____

d. _____

e. _____

f. _____

3. *The role of the Church and popes* _____

   a. _____

   b. _____

   c. _____

   d. _____

   e. _____

   f. _____

   g. _____

4. *The role of marriage and heredity* _____

   a. _____

   b. _____

   c. _____

B. *The Hundred Years War* _____

1. *Started by a succession dispute* _____

   a. _____

   b. _____

   c. _____

2. *New military technology* _____

   a. _____

b. _____

c. _____

d. _____

3. *Joan of Arc* _____

    a. _____

    b. _____

    c. _____

C. *New Monarchies in France and England* _____

1. *Both England and France consolidate* _____

    a. _____

    b. _____

    c. _____

2. *Noble resistance undermined by new military technology* _____

    a. _____

    b. _____

    c. _____

3. *Taxes on land and merchants* _____

    a. _____

    b. _____

    c. _____

4. *The Church also a source of revenue* _____

    a. _____

    b. _____

    c. _____

  5. *Representative bodies* _____

    a. _____

    b. _____

    c. _____

D. *Iberian Unification* _____

  1. *The reconquest of Iberia* _____

    a. _____

    b. _____

    c. _____

    d. _____

    e. _____

    f. _____

  2. *The reconquest of North Africa* _____

    a. _____

    b. _____

    c. _____

  3. *Ferdinand and Isabella, Granada, and Christopher Columbus* _____

    a. _____

    b. _____

    c. _____

VI. Conclusion

A. *Ecological successes and failures* _____

  1. _____

2. _____

3. _____

B. *1200–1500 represent a coming together of the basic features of the modern West* _____

   1. _____

   2. _____

   3. _____

C. *Ended a period of borrowing, on the threshold of expansion* _____

   1. _____

   2. _____

   3. _____

Identifications

Define each term and explain why it is significant, including any important dates.

	Identification	*Significance*
Latin West		
serfs		
three-field system		
Black Death		
water wheel		
mills		
Hanseatic League		
European Jews		

	Identification	*Significance*

guild

Gothic Cathedrals

Renaissance (European)

university

scholasticism

humanists (Renaissance)

printing press

Great Western Schism

Hundred Years War

new monarchies

reconquest of Iberia

Magna Carta

pollution

Multiple-Choice Questions

Read the entire question, including *all* the possible answers. Then choose the *one* answer that best fits the question.

1. Which of the following did *not* promote the Latin West's remarkable resurgence?
   a. Isolation
   b. Competition
   c. The pursuit of success
   d. The effective use of borrowed technology and learning

2. On average, how many hours per week did serfs spend laboring in their fields?
   a. Ninety-seven
   b. Sixty-three
   c. Fifty-four
   d. Thirty-two

3. Which of the following best explains Europe's population increase by 1300?
   a. The economy was reviving.
   b. Temperatures were warmer than usual.
   c. There were no severe epidemics.
   d. There is no best answer because historians just do not know for certain.

4. What most eased population pressure in Europe in the fourteenth century?
   a. Improved agricultural techniques
   b. Deaths caused by the Mongol invasions
   c. Migration to the Holy Land
   d. The Black Death

5. The first recorded antipollution law was passed by the British Parliament in
   a. 1388.
   b. 1960.
   c. 1842.
   d. 1066.

6. Most urban growth in the Latin West after 1200 stemmed from
   a. an influx of gold from Africa.
   b. the continuing growth of trade and manufacturing.
   c. the clearing of new farmland.
   d. improvements in breeding techniques of farm animals.

7. The Fourth Crusade was
   a. an attempt by Venetians to cripple Constantinople in order to gain better access to eastern trade.
   b. a last, futile attempt to hold on to the Holy Land.
   c. an attempt by the Holy Roman Emperor to take over the Byzantine Empire.
   d. deemed too costly and so was never executed.

8. Which of the following was the first to use heavy machinery in the production of paper?
   a. The Chinese
   b. The Muslims
   c. The Europeans
   d. The Africans

9. Latin European cities were able to adapt more quickly to changing market conditions than cities in China and the Islamic world because they were
   a. autonomous.
   b. under direct imperial control.
   c. controlled by the nobles.
   d. more numerous.

10. Which of the following was *not* an attribute of Gothic architecture?
    a. Round arches
    b. External or "flying" buttresses
    c. Great height
    d. Stained-glass windows

11. Modern historians see the Renaissance as
    a. a sudden break from the Dark Ages.
    b. less as a sudden break and more as the culmination of processes that were going on since medieval times.
    c. caused solely by the rediscovery of classical texts.
    d. caused solely by Muslim influence.

12. Which of the following did *not* contribute to the success of the new monarchies?
    a. The monarchs' success in controlling the power of their vassals
    b. The development of new weapons
    c. A closer relationship with the commercial elites
    d. A more competitive relationship with the church

13. Which of the following did *not* allow the new monarchs to make feudal knights relics of the past?
    a. The longbow
    b. The development of firearms
    c. More efficient financing of armies
    d. Improvements in armor

14. The Great Western Schism was finally resolved
    a. by the Protestant Reformation.
    b. by returning the pope to Rome, but Catholicism's political power was broken.
    c. by the Fourth Crusade against Constantinople.
    d. when the pope in Avignon died.

15. Which of the following did Ferdinand of Aragon and Isabella of Castile *not* gain in their takeover of Granada?
    a. A large population of Jewish bankers and merchants to help them finance Columbus's voyages
    b. Irrigated fields capable of producing an abundance of food
    c. Rich cities of glittering Moorish architecture
    d. Ports offering access to the Mediterranean and the South Atlantic

Short-Answer Questions

Answer each question in one short paragraph, giving the definition, dates, and significance.

1. How did serfdom slow improvements in agricultural production?

2. Discuss European attempts at agricultural expansion. Why was it attempted, what was the process involved, and how successful was it?

3. What two factors enabled the Italian city-states and Northern Europe to build such powerful trading empires in the Middle Ages? Explain.

4. Trace the growth of the Champagne Fairs. Why did they come about, how successful were they, and what caused them to decrease in importance?

5. Describe the institution of the university. How did it arise, and in what ways was it similar to or different from Islamic madrasa?

6. How did humanists and printers launch a revolution in the European world?

7. Discuss the attempt of King John of England at absolute control. Was he successful? Why, or why not?

8. What role did marriage play in royal succession?

Essay Questions

Make an outline for each question, listing the major points you want to discuss. Then write your practice essay, following your outline carefully and making sure that you do not skip any of your major points. At this time you will want to add the relevant dates and details that will make your essay persuasive and accurate.

1. Discuss the ecological effects of industry in medieval Europe.

2. Trace the growth of European industry, technology, and trade in the Middle Ages through the development of the textile industry.

3. Discuss the role of guilds, and explain how they functioned on a social, political, and economic level.

4. How did Europe benefit from cultural borrowing? From whom did they borrow and what was borrowed?

5. Discuss the relationship between monarchs, nobles, and the Church during the reigns of the new monarchs. Was this relationship different from that in feudal times? Why, or why not?

Comparison Charts

Using information gathered from the text, fill in the blank areas of each chart with the relevant data pertaining to the regions and categories listed. (Not all blank areas will necessarily be used.)

Chart 16.1
EUROPE'S FIRST INDUSTRIAL REVOLUTION: INDIGENOUS AND BORROWED ELEMENTS

	Agriculture	Transporta-tion and Navigation	Military	Mechanical Energy	Metallurgy and Mining	Navigation	Textiles	Paper and Printing	Math and Physics	Medicine	Education
Latin Europe: Late Middle Ages											
Latin Europe: Renaissance											
Influence from Byzantium											
Influence from Muslims											
Influence from China											

Chart 16.2
THE BLACK DEATH IN EUROPE

	Population	Symptoms and Life Expectancy	Psychological Effects	Resources	Economy and Labor	Government Response	Social Structure	Social Unrest
Pre-Plague Times								
Plague Years								
Recovery								

Society and Culture

After reading "Society and Culture: Blaming the Black Death on the Jews, Strasbourg, 1349" in your text, answer the following additional questions.

Jews died during the plague as well; how do you suppose the Christians of Strasbourg explained this? Do you think that some Christians were confused by the Pope's protection of the Jews in Avignon? How might they have explained that?

Internet Assignment

Keywords: "Gothic Cathedral"

"School of Athens"

While much of life for most people remained the same during the transition between the Middle Ages and the Renaissance, the world of ideas began to shift. Use the above keywords to find web sites about Gothic Cathedrals and Raphael's painting "School of Athens." You might want to consult the *History WIRED* image library on the Bulliet, *The Earth and Its Peoples* web site (refer to the preface of this study guide for information on how to locate the Bulliet home page).

How are Gothic Cathedrals representative of the late Middle Ages? How does Raphael's painting "School of Athens" represent the new ideas of the Renaissance? Can you find any similarities between the two works of art?

Internet Exploration

When you think of the European Middle Ages you probably think of King Arthur. In actuality many scholars think he may have lived as early as the fifth century C.E. (during the fall of the Western Roman Empire). Many scholars even think that Arthur was legendary. The reason we associate him with Medieval Europe is that stories about him were quite popular then. Use the keywords "King Arthur Legend" to find many fascinating web sites, and many different theories about Arthur. What evidence supports the theory that Arthur was an actual figure? Why might he be legendary? What made him so appealing to Europeans of the Middle Ages? What makes him so fascinating to us today?

Map Exercise

On Outline Map 16.1, shade in the course of the Black Death in these years, using different colors:

1347
1348
1349

1350
After 1350

Outline Map 16.1

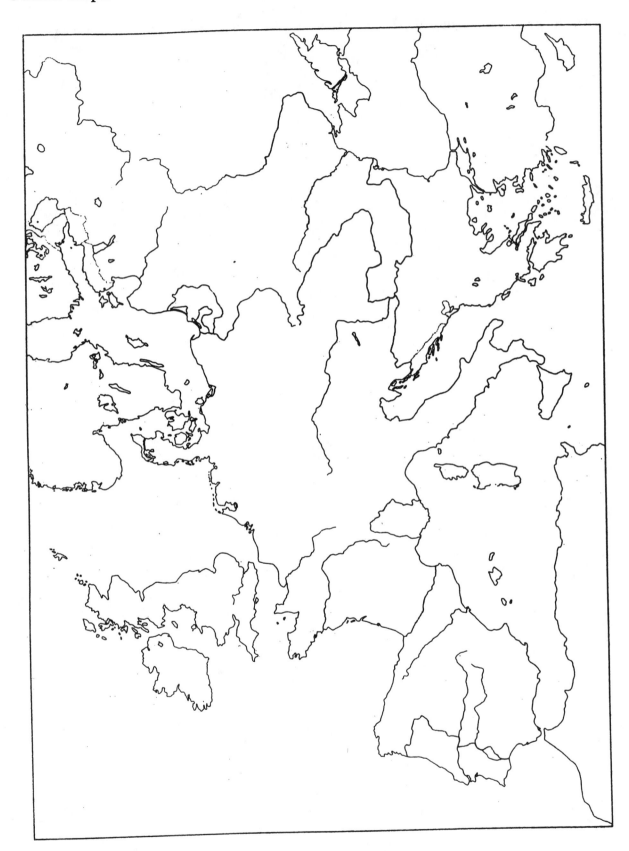

CHAPTER 17

The Maritime Revolution, to 1550

Learning Objectives

After reading Chapter 17 and completing this study chapter, you should be able to explain:

- In what ways the period from 1400 to 1550 represents a departure from earlier global expansion.

- Through what motives and methods Europeans gained global dominance.

- How the peoples of Africa, Asia, and the Americas reacted to European dominance.

- Why European empire building was more effective in the Americas than in either Africa or Asia.

Chapter Outline

In the outline below include important themes, concepts, and details in the blank spaces provided. If you find fewer points than you have space for, leave lines blank. If you find more points, add as many lines as necessary.

I. Introduction

    A. *Magellan's Voyages* _____

        1. _____

        2. _____

        3. _____

    B. *Completing the voyage* _____

        1. _____

2. _____

3. _____

C. *This was the end of an era in which influences tended to move from east to west* _____

    1. _____

    2. _____

    3. _____

II. **Global Maritime Expansion Before 1450**

  A. *The Pacific Ocean* _____

    1. *Peoples from Malay settled Southeast Asia* _____

      a. _____

      b. _____

      c. _____

    2. *Peoples from Fiji settled Polynesia* _____

      a. _____

      b. _____

      c. _____

    3. *Some scholars think they couldn't have done it except by accident—now we know it was planned* _____

      a. _____

      b. _____

      c. _____

  B. *The Indian Ocean* _____

    1. *Other Malayo-Indonesians* _____

      a. _____

b. _____

c. _____

2. *The rise of Medieval Islam boosted Indian Ocean trade* _____

   a. _____

   b. _____

   c. _____

3. *China and the Ming dynasty* _____

   a. _____

   b. _____

   c. _____

   d. _____

4. *Zheng He (1371–1435) and his voyages* _____

   a. _____

   b. _____

   c. _____

5. *Delegations from Africa* _____

   a. _____

   b. _____

   c. _____

6. *Opposition to voyages* _____

   a. _____

   b. _____

   c. _____

   d. _____

C.   *The Atlantic Ocean* _____

    1.   *The Vikings* _____

        a.   _____

        b.   _____

        c.   _____

        d.   _____

    2.   *Southern Europeans, Mediterranean, and the Atlantic Coast* _____

        a.   _____

        b.   _____

        c.   _____

    3.   *African voyages of exploration into the Atlantic* _____

        a.   _____

        b.   _____

        c.   _____

        d.   _____

        e.   _____

    4.   *Amerindians from South America* _____

        a.   _____

        b.   _____

        c.   _____

        d.   _____

III.   European Expansion, 1400–1550

A.   *Background to European Expansion* _____

1. *Motives* _____

   a. _____

   b. _____

   c. _____

2. *Methods* _____

   a. _____

   b. _____

   c. _____

B. *The Portuguese Voyages* _____

   1. *Prince Henry the Navigator* _____

      a. _____

      b. _____

      c. _____

   2. *Voyages* _____

      a. _____

      b. _____

      c. _____

   3. *Sailing far and returning* _____

      a. _____

      b. _____

      c. _____

      d. _____

   4. *Private enterprises made better progress* _____

      a. _____

b. _____

c. _____

d. _____

C. *The Spanish Voyages* _____

   1. *Columbus* _____

      a. _____

      b. _____

      c. _____

   2. *Amerigo Vespucci explored American mainland* _____

      a. _____

      b. _____

      c. _____

   3. *1454—Treaty of Tordesillas with Portugal* _____

      a. _____

      b. _____

      c. _____

   4. *Balboa and Magellan* _____

      a. _____

      b. _____

      c. _____

IV. Encounters with Europe, 1450–1550

A. *Western Africa* _____

   1. *Gold Coast—eager for trade with the Portuguese* _____

a. _____

b. _____

c. _____

2. *Early contact mixed commercial, military, and religious interests* _____

    a. _____

    b. _____

    c. _____

3. *Benin—near the peak of its power when first encountering the Portuguese* _____

    a. _____

    b. _____

    c. _____

4. *Kongo* _____

    a. _____

    b. _____

    c. _____

    d. _____

B. *Eastern Africa* _____

1. *1498—Malindi* _____

    a. _____

    b. _____

    c. _____

2. *Christian Ethiopia* _____

    a. _____

b. _____

c. _____

3. *African encounters with the Portuguese before 1550 varied considerably* _____

   a. _____

   b. _____

   c. _____

C. *Indian Ocean States* _____

   1. *1498—da Gama arrived at Malabar Coast* _____

      a. _____

      b. _____

      c. _____

   2. *Portuguese wanted a private "Portuguese Sea"* _____

      a. _____

      b. _____

      c. _____

      d. _____

      e. _____

   3. *Portuguese power grab and resistance* _____

      a. _____

      b. _____

      c. _____

      d. _____

      e. _____

D. *The Americas*

    1. *Territorial rather than trading empire*

        a. _____

        b. _____

        c. _____

    2. *Aztecs—leader Moctezuma II*

        a. _____

        b. _____

        c. _____

        d. _____

        e. _____

    3. *Inca—leader Atahualpa*

        a. _____

        b. _____

        c. _____

E. *Patterns of Dominance*

    1. *European dominance more complete in Americas due to*

        a. _____

        b. _____

        c. _____

        d. _____

    2. *Less successful in Old World*

        a. _____

        b. _____

c. _____

d. _____

V. Conclusion

A. *Century between 1450 and 1550 a turning point in world history—modern age* _____

1. _____

2. _____

3. _____

B. *Degree of conquest similar to some that had gone before* _____

1. _____

2. _____

3. _____

C. *European empires lasted longer and had a bigger impact* _____

1. _____

2. _____

3. _____

Identifications

Define each term and explain why it is significant, including any important dates.

	Identification	*Significance*
Zheng He		
Arawak		
Henry the Navigator		
caravel		

Identification   *Significance*

Gold Coast

Treaty of Tordesillas

Bartolomeu Dias

Vasco da Gama

Christopher Columbus

Ferdinand Magellan

Kongo

Malindi

Christian Ethiopia

Malacca

conquistadors

Hernán Cortés

Moctezuma

Francisco Pizarro

Atahualpa

Multiple-Choice Questions

Read the entire question, including *all* the possible answers. Then choose the *one* answer that best fits the question.

1. The *Victoria*'s successful return to Spain in 1522 was
   a. the signal that the Spanish were not to be the dominant force in the Americas.
   b. the crowning example of the Europeans' new ability and determination to make themselves masters of the oceans.
   c. the end of the first expedition led by the English.
   d. the final glory of Spanish dominance in Asia.

2. The Polynesian migrations were
   a. obviously accidental since Polynesians lacked navigational devices to plot their way.
   b. obviously from the Americas as Thor Heyerdhal proved in 1947.
   c. the result of a planned expansion.
   d. really a small and unimpressive achievement.

3. Why did the Viking settlements of Greenland and Vinland go into decline after 1200?
   a. The weather changed.
   b. Those colonies seceded.
   c. The Vikings' attention was drawn to continental affairs.
   d. The mainland Vikings became Christians, but the island Vikings did not, causing a breach between the two groups.

4. Why did the Iberians begin making the voyages of exploration?
   a. To reach Eastern markets
   b. To find a route to the Americas
   c. To relieve population pressure at home
   d. To find a market for surplus goods produced by the Industrial Revolution

5. Which of the following was *not* one aspect of the Portuguese attack on Ceuta in 1415?
   a. A plundering expedition
   b. A religious crusade
   c. A military tournament
   d. A diplomatic overture

6. The Treaty of Tordesillas (1494)
   a. split the world between Spain and Portugal.
   b. legalized African slave trading.
   c. protected Amerindians from Spanish abuses.
   d. was vetoed by the pope.

7. When the Portuguese first encountered African kingdoms
   a. they found nothing of interest there.
   b. they were equal in power, or even less powerful than their African counterparts.
   c. they easily dominated them.
   d. they found that Africans had no interest in trade.

8. What finally kept Portugal and Ethiopia from making a permanent alliance?
    a. The Portuguese were afraid to make an alliance with a Muslim kingdom.
    b. Ethiopia needed military assistance that the Portuguese were unwilling to give.
    c. Ethiopia was led by a Queen, and Christian countries were never led by female monarchs.
    d. Ethiopia refused to transfer Christian affiliation from the patriarch of Alexandria to the pope in Rome.

9. Which of the following probably was *not* a motivating factor in the Ming voyages of exploration?
    a. Curiosity
    b. Enhancing commerce
    c. Desire for a territorial empire
    d. Enhancing other people's awe of Ming power and achievements

10. The new anti-Muslim Crusades of 1396 and 1444 were launched by the Europeans because
    a. of a renaissance in European Christianity.
    b. the Europeans had finally made contact with the elusive Prester John, and he was going to help reclaim the Holy Land.
    c. the expansion of the Ottoman Turks disrupted trade routes.
    d. they felt the need to compete with the Chinese in their voyages of exploration.

11. Columbus finally persuaded Queen Isabella and King Ferdinand to finance his voyage to the East Indies by
    a. impressing them with his command of geography.
    b. offering a money-back guarantee.
    c. proving his theory by using a ninth-century Arab map.
    d. sheer persistence.

12. Why did Columbus call the native people of the Americas "Indians"?
    a. He thought that he had landed on an island in the East Indies.
    b. He thought that he had landed in India.
    c. *Indian* was a word meaning foreigner.
    d. *Indian* was a word meaning savage.

13. The Portuguese were able to assert control over the Indian Ocean because
    a. of the superiority of Christianity over indigenous beliefs.
    b. the constant warfare in the region allowed the disruption of traditional trade systems.
    c. Portuguese trade goods were vastly superior to anything to be found in the region.
    d. of the superiority of their ships and weapons over the smaller and lightly armed merchant dhows.

14. How did the Arawaks respond to the Spaniards' ever-increasing demands for more gold?
    a. They gladly provided more of their plentiful gold.
    b. They told Columbus exaggerated stories about gold in other places to persuade him to move on.
    c. They ran away.
    d. They held Columbus for ransom in order to get gold from the Spaniards.

15. Which of the following factors did *not* contribute to the success of the Spanish in creating a vast land empire so quickly in the Americas?
    a. Spaniards immigrated in great numbers to the American colonies.
    b. The long isolation of the Americas made its inhabitants vulnerable to European diseases.
    c. The Spanish had superior military technology.
    d. The Spaniards' conquest of the Americas was patterned after their already proven success in reconquering Granada.

Short-Answer Questions

Answer each question in one short paragraph, giving the definition, dates, and significance.

1. Why did the Ming voyages of exploration end?

2. What kind of technology was employed by the Portuguese, and later other Europeans, to facilitate their voyages of exploration?

3. What did Alfonso I hope to gain by his relationship with the Portuguese and how did the situation get out of his control?

4. Why did Ethiopia need Portuguese help and under what conditions would Portugal grant it?

5. Describe the career, motivation, and impact of Prince Henry the Navigator.

6. Briefly explain why the century between 1450 and 1550 was a major turning point in history.

Essay Questions

Make an outline of each question, listing the major points you want to discuss. Then write your practice essay, following your outline carefully and making sure that you do not skip any of your major points. At this time you will want to add the relevant dates and details that will make your essay persuasive and accurate.

1. Briefly describe the non-European patterns of expansion before 1450. What were the goals in these expansions and what methods were used to achieve them?

2. What were the Europeans' motives and methods in their voyages of exploration?

3. Compare and contrast three responses to European exploration.

4. Describe the role of the Portuguese in the Indian Ocean trading network. What methods did they use and how successful were they in achieving their goals?

5. Why were Europeans so much more successful in establishing territorial empires in the Americas than in Africa and Asia?

Comparison Charts

Using information gathered from the text, fill in the blank areas of each chart with the relevant data pertaining to the regions and categories listed. (Not all blank areas will necessarily be used.)

Chart 17.1
PATTERNS OF EXPANSION

	Dates	Regions	Goals	Technology	Impact
Spanish/ Portuguese					
Mongol					
Chinese					
Muslim					
Malayo-Indonesian					
Amerindian					

Chart 17.2
EUROPEAN IMPACT IN ASIA AND AFRICA VERSUS IMPACT IN AMERICA

	Asia/Africa	America
Motives		
Methods		
Response by Local Peoples		

Society and Culture

After reading "Society and Culture: European Male Sexual Dominance" in your text, answer the following additional questions.

How might native women and their children have benefited through their close association with the European conquerors? What disadvantages might they have encountered with members of their own culture?

Internet Assignment

Keywords: "Psalter world map"

                         "Henricus Martellus map" or "Cantino world map"

Maps are valuable tools we use to locate streets, schools, and vacation spots. But maps can also be used to learn about the people who created them. Use the above keywords to locate web sites about the Psalter world map, Henricus Martellus map, and the Cantino world map. You might want to consult the *History WIRED* image library on the Bulliet, *The Earth and Its Peoples* web site (refer to the preface of this study guide for information on how to locate the Bulliet home page).

The first keyword is for a map from the Middle Ages, and the second set of keywords is for maps from the early Renaissance period. What do you notice about the map from the Middle Ages? What is missing? How do the Renaissance maps differ in style and geography from the Medieval maps? What seems to be the major concern of each map? What do you think of the geographical accuracy of these maps? How does each map reflect the outlook of the people who created them?

Internet Exploration

Today with modern jets, satellites, and transatlantic conference calls, it's hard to imagine that long, dangerous voyages were once the only way to see the world. But in the 16th century the only way to travel was on wooden oceangoing vessels with uncertain navigational techniques. To learn something about how we used to travel use the keyword "history of the caravel," or you might like to try the specific web site http://www.ruf.rice.edu/~feefi/site_map.html (be sure to look at the "Science of Navigation" section). Would you like to have been alive in those days, sailing into unknown lands? What adventures and perils might you have encountered?

Map Exercises

On Outline Map 17.1, plot the routes of the following:

Voyages of Zheng He
Polynesian voyages
Malayo-Indonesian voyages
African voyages
Prince Henry the Navigator's ships

Christopher Columbus
Vasco Da Gama
Amerigo Vespucci
Ferdinand Magellan

On Outline Map 17.2, use shading to differentiate the following:

Aztec Empire
Inca Empire
Arawak homeland
Arawak voyages

Carib voyages
Andean voyages

Outline Map 17.1

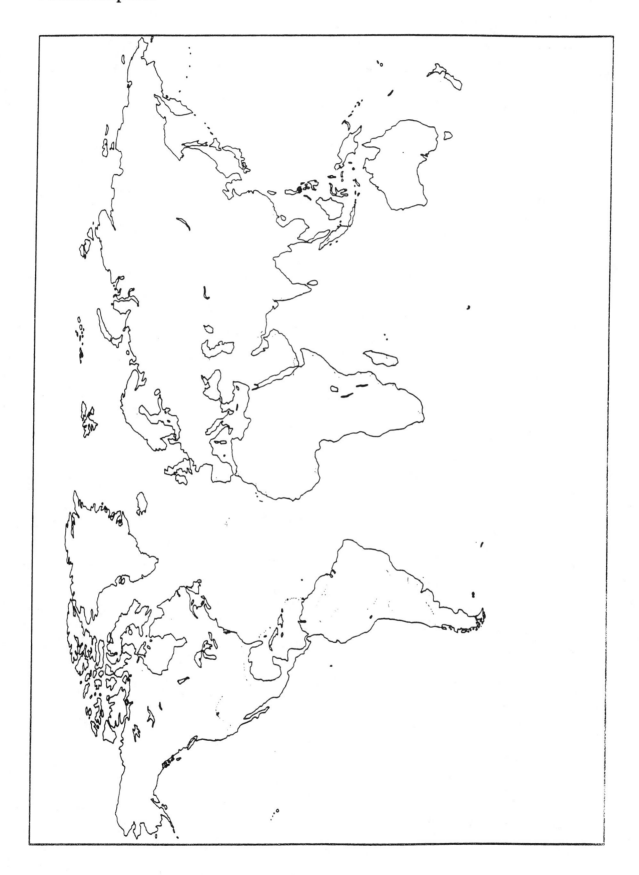

Outline Map 17.2

Answers to the Multiple-Choice Questions

Chapter 1

1. b
2. b
3. c
4. a
5. c
6. c
7. b
8. c
9. c
10. b
11. c
12. b
13. a
14. a
15. d

Chapter 2

1. a
2. b
3. b
4. a
5. a
6. c
7. a
8. a
9. d
10. b
11. c
12. b
13. a
14. d
15. c
16. a

Chapter 3

1. d
2. d
3. b
4. d
5. c
6. a
7. c
8. b
9. b
10. a
11. a
12. a
13. a
14. d

Chapter 4

1. b
2. a
3. d
4. b
5. d
6. a
7. c
8. a
9. b
10. a
11. a
12. c
13. a
14. b
15. b
16. d

Chapter 5

1. b
2. d
3. c
4. a
5. a
6. c
7. c
8. b
9. a
10. a
11. b
12. d
13. c
14. d
15. b

Chapter 6

1. b
2. c
3. d
4. a
5. c
6. c
7. b
8. c
9. c
10. c
11. b
12. c
13. b
14. c
15. d
16. a
17. c

Chapter 7

1. b
2. a
3. b
4. d
5. b
6. c
7. a
8. a
9. b
10. b
11. d
12. b
13. c
14. a
15. d

Chapter 8

1. a
2. c
3. b
4. a
5. d
6. c
7. a
8. d
9. b
10. b
11. a
12. b
13. c
14. a
15. b

Chapter 9

1. a
2. d
3. b
4. a
5. b
6. c
7. d
8. b
9. d
10. b
11. a
12. a

Chapter 10

1. b
2. a
3. c
4. a
5. c
6. b
7. b
8. b
9. a
10. b
11. a
12. b
13. d

Chapter 11

1. b
2. a
3. b
4. c
5. a
6. d

7. b
8. b
9. a
10. d
11. d
12. d
13. c
14. c
14. a

Chapter 12

1. a
2. c
3. a
4. b
5. a
6. c
7. b
8. c
9. d
10. a
11. c
12. d
13. d
14. b

Chapter 13

1. b
2. a
3. d
4. d
5. c
6. a
7. d
8. d
9. a
10. a

11. a
12. c
13. c

Chapter 14

1. a
2. c
3. d
4. a
5. c
6. a
7. b
8. d
9. a
10. b
11. a
12. b
13. c
14. c
14. c

Chapter 15

1. b
2. c
3. a
4. c
5. b
6. a
7. d
8. b
9. c
10. a
11. c
12. c
13. a
15. b
16. c

17. b
15. c
15. b

Chapter 16

1. a
2. c
3. d
4. d
5. a
6. b
7. a
8. c
9. a
10. a
11. b
12. d
13. d
14. b
15. a

Chapter 17

1. b
2. c
3. a
4. a
5. d
6. a
7. b
8. d
9. c
10. c
11. d
12. a
13. d
14. b
15. a